A LIFETIME IN THE BUSH:
THE BIOGRAPHY OF LEN BEADELL

by Mark Shephard

Other books by the author Mark Shephard
  Aviculture in Australia
  The Simpson Desert – Natural History and human endeavour
  The Great Victoria Desert – north of the Nullarbor, south of the Centre

Cover design MoBros, Adelaide
Photomontage, main photograph
of Gary Highway,
Courtesy, Peter Vernon.

A LIFETIME IN THE BUSH:
THE BIOGRAPHY OF LEN BEADELL

by Mark Shephard

GECKO
BOOKS

Shephard, Mark
A lifetime in the bush : the biography of Len Beadell

ISBN 978-1-876247-04-1 (paperback)

1. Beadell, Len, 1923-1995. 2. Surveyors - Australia - Biography. 3. Authors - Australia - Biography. 4. Woomera (S. Aust.) I. Title.

526.9092

Designed by David Hayes, Lofty Designs, Longwood, SA 5153
Printed by Hyde Park Press, Richmond, SA 5033
First published in 1998 by Corkwood Press.

Reprinted 1998, 2000, 2003
Reprinted 2009 by Gecko Books

GECKO
BOOKS

PO Box 118
Marleston
South Australia 5033

Telephone 08 8351 1688

A R T S A   This project has been assisted by the South Australian
Government through Arts SA

CONTENTS

FOREWORD

L EN BEADELL played a vital role in enabling all Australians to experience the real outback by building his incredible network of roads under the toughest conditions imaginable. Only those who have travelled Len's highways can appreciate how stark, beautiful and isolated the deserts can be.

He was a pioneer. After his wartime experience in Papua New Guinea, he returned to Australia eager to become involved in projects which would, in some way, change the face of his country. Len Beadell's legacy to Australia is the network of roads that he first charted in the outback, guided by the stars. He and his team built more than 6 000 km of roads over a period of eight years and for the first time opened up vast areas of Australia's harsh interior.

Len conquered the isolation of the outback, but thoughts of his family were never far away. The Anne Beadell Highway, the Connie Sue Highway, the Gary Highway and Jackie Junction are all named after his wife and children. These roads, as well as Len's famous Gunbarrel Highway, have made the outback accessible to everyone.

Len and his family came to stay with Pip and I in 1994 when we were proud to award him the *Australian Geographic* Adventurer of the Year Gold Medallion. I found him to be the most wonderful unassuming person.

I haven't driven the Gunbarrel Highway – but I have flown along it in my Bell Jetranger helicopter. We had lunch, with the helicopter parked on the highway, at the midway point near Mt Beadell. I hadn't seen a car all day and just as we started putting the Vegemite on the bread, a vehicle arrived. The occupants had to drive out around us, which wasn't too difficult – there's plenty of room to manoeuvre in the Gibson Desert.

I also had the pleasure of accompanying Len on the first Bourke to Burketown Bash, a car trial which I started to raise money for the Variety Club of Australia. Len was a wonderful travelling companion, supplying us with anecdotes around the campfire.

In 1995 I asked *Australian Geographic* to assist in locating the bulldozer Len used to construct the Gunbarrel Highway. It was eventually tracked down to a property 100km south of Perth. I am now in the process of having the bulldozer restored to its original working condition to preserve an important piece of Australian history.

Mark has written a wonderful book which I believe any person who calls himself or herself a true Australian should read.

Dick Smith

AUTHOR'S NOTE AND ACKNOWLEDGMENTS

THE writing of Len Beadell's biography has been somewhat of a daunting task. How does one do justice to a man who achieved so much and had such a profound impact on so many Australians? I should state clearly from the outset that, in writing Len's biography, it was never my intention to try to duplicate Len's own unique and humorous style of writing. To do so, I believe, would be a total injustice to Len. Rather, I have tried simply to relate Len's life story in chronological sequence, placing particular emphasis on his pre- and post- road-building days and endeavouring to fill in the gaps about Len's life. Len himself disliked loose ends and I know he wanted his life story to be tidied up. This book aims to do so.

The first four chapters of the book detail Len's childhood and early surveying days in Papua New Guinea and the Top End of Australia. Len and I discussed this period of his life in a series of taped interviews conducted at his home. I have written this section of the book fundamentally as it was told to me by Len.

Chapters 5 to 7 of the book describes Len's halcyon road-building days and his involvement in the British Nuclear Testing Programme. I have presented this key period of Len's life in a way that does not simply rework his own writings.

The latter chapters of the book contain a series of personal recollections about Len from both his family and a number of people who were particularly close to him. The final section of the book provides a number of facts and figures about Len's life and work, many of which have never been documented.

I have introduced Len's own spoken words or writings into the telling of his life story at various points in the book. The transcript of Len's 'standard bush lecture' in Chapter 6, which he presented to around 940 audiences around Australia, provides a lasting opportunity for readers to continue to enjoy Len's humour. Chapter 9 gives an account of Len's overseas exploits in 1959. A number of Len's trademark illustrations are interspersed throughout the text: most of these have never been published.

The writing of a book is always a team effort, requiring the help of many people. Len's biography has been no different. I wish to thank the Beadell family, notably Anne and Connie for their untiring efforts in providing me with a constant stream of information. Connie has shown a vigorous enthusiasm for this project and an admirable determination to keep the memory of her father's achievements alive and well.

I say a collective thank you to Len's sister Phyllis, Rex Ellis, Dr Bryan Gatehouse, John Harrison, Norman Hetherington, David Hewitt, Dr Leon Hoare, Marie Mahood, Dick Lang, Reg Munyard, Dean Nicolle, Doug Stoneham, Peter Vernon, Peter Wenham, Kevin Whisson, Dr John Whitehouse and Howell Witt, all of whom have contributed their personal thoughts about Len. Others including John Coles, Bina Stone, David Field, Anthony Beresford, Ann and John Draper, Ray Meldrum, Yasmin Neal and Rob Wetselaar provided additional information on Len's life.

A special thanks is extended to the people of the Ngaanyatjarra Lands and Frank Young (on behalf of the Watarru Community, Anangu Pitjantjatara Council) who gave permission to reproduce photographs taken on their Lands.

David Hayes, Lofty Designs, drew the maps and designed the book. Beryl Mazzachi, Chris Wenham and Peter Vernon provided photographic assistance. Unless otherwise credited, the photos presented are taken from the Beadell family albums and Len's slide collection. To Lesley Hutton who has been my typist since day one of my writing career, thanks once again for another splendid effort. I know you enjoyed typing Len's story. I would particularly like to record my special thanks to Arts SA, Adelaide, for their assistance in writing this book.

Finally to my wife Anne and my children Matthew and Emily – you continue to be an inspiration in my life. Thank you for your limitless patience.

Mark Shephard,
Adelaide.

Introduction

A PERSONAL TRIBUTE TO LEN BEADELL

T HE first rays of sunlight flickered above the horizon in the Gibson Desert. It was one of those typically crisp winter mornings in the Australian outback. For the past half an hour I had been attempting in vain to relight our campfire with twigs, sticks and matches. Suddenly a giant figure, with beefy legs as tough as weathered buffalo hide and clad in baggy khaki shorts, shuffled across the camp. He kicked the ashes with the side of his hob-nailed boots and the morning fire was away in an instant.

'What a wondrous morning,' sparkled Len with a trademark toothy grin. Len greeted every morning in the desert with the same breezy enthusiasm.

We were camped at the base of Mt Leisler on the Sandy Blight Junction Road. The explorer William Henry Tietkens named this prominent bluff on 27 May 1889. Tietkens, who at the time was in command of the Central Australian Exploring Expedition, also blazed a tree at the base of Mt Leisler.

As the sun rose slightly higher above the horizon, burnishing the impressive eastern escarpment of Mt Leisler, I stood at this historic tree with Len Beadell. I listened intently as Len described the story of how he deliberately directed the Sandy Blight Junction Road right past this landmark in June 1960. I pondered how fortunate my family and I were to be on a private desert trip with the man who had opened up 2.5 million square kilometres of the Great Victoria, Gibson, Little Sandy and Great Sandy Deserts (the so-called Western Deserts of outback Australia) some 35 years earlier; and my mind flashed back to my first encounter with Len.

For many years throughout my childhood and early adult years, I had yearned to travel the Australian deserts and enjoy their natural, cultural and historic riches. But could I handle the

1

Mark Shepbard

Tietkens' Tree near
the base of Mt Leisler
on the Sandy Blight
Junction Road.

vagaries of the desert and how could I ever get there? At that stage, I didn't own a four-wheel-drive vehicle. I was leisurely flicking through the pages of the Adelaide *Advertiser* one Saturday morning early in 1988. I came across an advertisement for a desert safari organised by Adelaide-based tour operator Dick Lang to commemorate the 30th Anniversary of the completion of the Gunbarrel Highway, Len Beadell's most well-known outback road. That same night, I attended a lecture given by Len at a local community centre. Tears of laughter streamed down my face as I listened to Len tell stories about the establishment of Woomera, the history of the British Nuclear Testing Programme at Emu and Maralinga, and the building of his network of desert roads. And it wasn't only me who enjoyed hearing Len talk. During the preparation of this book, my typist and long-time friend, Lesley Hutton, transcribed the tape of a similar lecture given by Len some years later. She remarked that it was the funniest and most enjoyable piece of work she had typed in 20 years of professional work!

I was hooked on Len Beadell after that talk and immediately passed over my silver coins to Dick Lang to secure my place on that 30th Anniversary trip.

In what seemed like an instant later, I was heading off to the Gibson and Great Victoria Deserts in April 1988 with 14 other passengers. It was my first chance to personally meet Len and Anne Beadell, who were special guests on that trip. My initial impressions of Len centred on how warm and friendly he was to each and every passenger. We were all virtually complete strangers to Len, but he (and Anne) made a deliberate effort to talk to us individually and in a private moment.

At that stage, I was contemplating writing my first book. Len showed genuine enthusiasm and excitement for this project. He himself had authored six books. Yet he didn't want to talk to me about his books. He was totally focussed on learning more about my intended work. I have never forgotten that discussion with Len, as it provided me with the self-belief and impetus to launch my writing career.

After thundering down the Gunbarrel Highway during the day, we all looked forward to hearing Len vividly recount his road building exploits around the campfire at night. He commanded our attention. His cackling, infectious laugh held us spellbound. He was the pre-eminent bush raconteur. By the time he had finished with us, we all drifted off to our tents with a broad smile on our faces.

I became captivated with Len's ability to recall the most minuscule details about dates, times, places and events which had occurred some three and a half decades earlier. I soon learned that, beyond his free-spirited attitude and sharp-witted humour, Len was a truly caring person, a deep thinker, and a man of practical, creative and precise mind.

The hardships endured by Len and his road-building team (the now-legendary Gunbarrel Road Construction Party) were immense. There were extremes of intense heat and cold, red clouds of dust, black clouds of blowflies, innumerable mechanical breakdowns, and seemingly never-ending battles with mountainous sandridges and limitless spinifex plains. Yet Len was perfect as leader of the Gunbarrel Road Construction Party. To him, urban life was decidedly claustrophobic and he craved the endless horizons of the bush. And his meticulous skills as a surveyor in the most formidable of conditions guaranteed the success of every bush project he was asked to undertake. His surveying skills had been honed immaculately over 30 years, initially under the guidance of his scoutmaster and mentor, John Richmond and later in the jungles of New Guinea during World War II, as a member of the army's Eighth Survey Corps. He later worked in the wilds of Arnhem Land as surveyor with the first scientific expedition into that region.

But back to the trip. We were heading west past the spectacular Rawlinson Range after leaving the Giles Weather Station. One of the passengers said to Len: 'It must be good to be in the bush again.' Len replied laconically: 'We're not in the bush yet!' And for the next hundred kilometres or so, the two-way repartee between Len and the passengers continued as to whether we were indeed in the bush. We stopped at Mt Samuel in the Gibson Desert. Len led us to its summit from where I witnessed the most inspiring desert vista imaginable – thick mulga woodland extending as far as the eye could see in every direction. The sense of open space was exhilarating and over-whelming. Len remarked: 'Now we're finally in the bush!'

We soon passed Mt Beadell, the most enduring landmark to Len's desert exploits. Later that day we camped near Mungilli Claypan. After consuming Dick's 'Carnegie Curry' for dinner, it was party time. Len, Anne and Dick had chosen this location to celebrate the 30th Anniversary of the completion of the Gunbarrel Highway. Champagne corks were popped and a cake – decorated with a replica of the Gunbarrel grader – was devoured. It was a night to remember for all concerned. Indeed the camaraderie among our group, directly fostered by Len, remained well after this trip. For years later, we religiously held an annual reunion of the '30th Anniversary mob.' Len had a special ability to bond people from all walks of life.

After surviving my first desert experience, I, like Len, was totally consumed with passion for the Australian deserts. I bought that four-wheel-drive and my family and I have journeyed across most of Len's roads over the past decade. 1991 was particularly memorable because we had the opportunity to travel on a private trip with the Beadells and their daughter Connie. Long-time friends, George and Ruth Aspley, also Beadell followers, accompanied us on our trip which encompassed the Anne Beadell Highway, the Connie Sue Highway north to Warburton, and from there onto Giles, the Sandy Blight Junction Road, and the Gary Junction Road.

We had a theme for this trip. Len really enjoyed going bush for a particular purpose. We were looking for a rare bird, the scarlet-chested parrot or 'red-winged condor', as Len jovially called it. We never found the bird on this trip (we did several years later). But it didn't matter. We were all grateful for sharing the experience of having our own private guided tour of the Western Deserts with Len. We revelled in his company.

Throughout the ensuing chapters of this book, Len is described variously as the Pied Piper, the Gentle Giant of the Bush, and the Iron Man of the Inland. He was all those things. Regarding the first-mentioned, I'll never forget pulling up at an Aboriginal community near the Western Australian/Northern Territory border. Two dozen Aboriginal children swarmed around Len like bees at a honeypot. And then an Aboriginal man in his late thirties walked up to Len and shook his hand. The man had not seen Len for 30 years, but was obviously overjoyed to renew his acquaintance. It seemed everyone in the bush knew Len Beadell.

Well, not quite everybody! Len accidentally gashed his knee later during the trip. The wound required medical attention. We duly arrived at Warburton and Anne, Ruth and I took Len to the Community Hospital. A well-meaning nurse examined Len and began to take down some details. 'Your surname?' asked the

In the bush at last – the view from the top of Mt Samuel in the Gibson Desert.

A majestic ghost gum near Gill's Pinnacle in the Schwerin Mural Crescent.

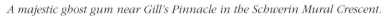

nurse. 'Beadell,' replied Len. 'How do you spell that?' enquired the nurse. We were totally dumbfounded. Here was someone working right in the heart of Beadell country who didn't know Len. Len just laughed it off in typical fashion. As it turned out, the nurse had only been at Warburton for two weeks, after being seconded from Perth. She was excused!

Soon after leaving Warburton, we made an enforced stop to repair several tyres which had been punctured by mulga stakes. All desert travellers will know only too well that flat tyres can cause infuriating delays to bush itineraries. Len himself had painstakingly mended thousands of tyres during his road building days. Yet, here again, Len was in his element, calmly offering useful advice, lending a helping hand, and showing extraordinary patience and tolerance towards others. I'd seen Len behave in exactly the same manner on our 1988 Gunbarrel safari, when a series of staked tyres caused major delays in the latter part of that trip.

We pushed on to perhaps my favourite location in the Western Desert country, the Schwerin Mural Crescent, north-east of Giles. This picturesque line of purple hills, adorned with stately, gleaming-white ghost gums, was named in 1874 by the erstwhile explorer Ernest Giles, whose epic feats and romantic writings were equally admired by Len and myself.

Len aligned the southern end of the Sandy Blight Junction Road close to the Schwerin Mural Crescent, as part of what he proudly called his 'road beautification scheme'. Wherever there is an important landmark or scenic geographical feature in the Western Deserts, be rest assured that, where practical, Len built a road right alongside it. He had the foresight to understand that others would follow his bush tracks and he wanted to ensure that desert travellers saw the very best the outback could offer.

We stopped close to Gill's Pinnacle, the most prominent feature in the Schwerin Mural Crescent. Len removed an axe from the back of his Toyota, walked across to a nearby ghost gum, and proceeded with great gusto to chop away at a blaze in the tree bearing one of his trademark aluminium plaques. Len regularly undertook careful restoration work on his desert signposts

Wood chips fly as Len Beadell undertakes restoration work at one of his bush signposts.

throughout our trip.   He was keen for them to remain as significant historical features of the desert landscape.

Giles Creek and Rebecca Creek were soon encountered. These delightful red gum-lined creeks are of special significance to my family.   My son Matthew's third name is Giles and my daughter Emily's middle name is Rebecca.   As six-month-old Matthew played in the sandy bed of Giles Creek, we enjoyed a mouth-watering camp oven roast among the ghostly desert oaks nearby. I leaned back in my bush chair and hoped that my children would come to appreciate and understand why we chose these names for them; and that they too would have the opportunity to travel the Beadell Tracks in their later lives.

The following day our small convoy came to a sudden halt along the Sandy Blight Junction Road, in what seemed the middle of nowhere.   The surrounding country was flat and appeared totally devoid of discernible landmarks.   Len hustled us out of our vehicles and eagerly pointed out a series of Aboriginal rockholes

An impressive Aboriginal rockhole along the Sandy Blight Junction Road.

Mark Shephard

in a low granite outcrop which had not been visible from the road. Circular patterns, indicating water, were inscribed into the rockface, as was an arrowhead pointing to the location of the rockhole itself. This experience reinforced to us yet again that Len knew the desert country intimately, literally inch by inch.

Our weary party eventually came out of the desert via the Gary Junction Road, another of Len's outback tracks which bears the name of a Beadell family member, son Gary.

The final part of our journey incorporated a brief trip to the Simpson Desert. We visited the waddy trees on the western edge of the Simpson. Len had never seen this rare stand of trees, some of which were up to 500 years-old. He was excited. At last I had the opportunity to repay Len in some small way for the pleasure he had given my family and I on our travels across the Beadell Tracks.

And, in writing his biography, it is my aim to perpetuate the memory of Len Beadell for many years to come. I'll never forget the day I visited Len at his home in April 1995 to continue our discussions about his biography. Len was clearly unwell. His grandson, Mitchell, touched him on his knee and, with a concerned expression, asked: 'Are you all right, Lenny?' Unfortunately Len was not all right.

Len's family have given me their blessing to continue and

complete Len's life story. For that, I thank them sincerely. Len often remarked that it was a privilege to be able to work in the outback and be responsible for opening up Australia's interior. I say it has been my privilege to be able to document the life story of a truly remarkable Australian, whose spirit will live forever in the Australian deserts.

Mark Shephard

Chapter 1

GRASSROOTS

IT was mid 1870 when Edwin and Marie Beadell (Len's paternal grandparents) left England and headed for a new life on Australian shores. Edwin was a successful antique appreciator and collector in London, but he decided to head to Australia to establish a new importing and indenting business in Hunter Street, Sydney. Indenting involved the importation of light polo ponies to Australia from English studs. The Beadells initially resided at Mosman in a stately house called Woodlands; in addition to the house, they bought four large blocks of land in the heart of Lane Cove, which were rented to local business people. Four children were born to the family – Frank, Olive, Ivy and Fred Algernon (Len's father). The children were educated at North Shore Sydney Grammar School. From his very young days, Fred developed a love of the bush and his parents subsequently enrolled him in the Wagga Wagga Agricultural College. Here he learnt the basics of agriculture and animal husbandry.

After Fred graduated from the college, his parents decided to send him to Redcliffe sheep station near Cunnamulla, 800 kilometres west of Brisbane. Edwin knew the owner of Redcliffe, Fritz Frith, who was prepared to give Fred a job and 'knock the lad into shape.'

Fred left home with a leather carry bag, stockwhip and an 1892 Winchester 12-gauge shotgun, which was a present from his father. This walnut-butted rifle later became a treasured possession of Len's and it hung proudly on the lounge wall of his family's Salisbury home for many years.

Fred worked long days on Redcliffe Station droving over 500 sheep with his trusty sheepdog, Smoky. His strong work ethic and no-nonsense approach stood him in good stead for hard station life and his horsemanship soon became renowned in the

Len's father (standing, far right, arms folded) at Redcliffe Station, 1906.

district. Over the course of the next five years, Fred gradually worked his way up to overseer of Redcliffe Station.

In 1910 a young nurse from Townsville, Viola Pearl Mackay, visited Redcliffe for a short holiday. Viola's family were well-known throughout north Queensland. Her father, Herbert Mackay, was the district's Surveyor General; he placed the trigonometric station on Castle Hill overlooking Townsville and spent months at a time surveying the north Queensland coast in his horse and dray. Viola, the youngest of the Mackay's nine children (six girls and three boys) was introduced to Fred soon after her arrival at Redcliffe. In Len's words: 'They met up, they seemed to click and that was that.' After a short courtship, Fred Beadell left Redcliffe Station and went to Townsville where he married Viola Mackay on 19 December 1914 at St James Cathedral.

Both were 25 years of age at the time. As a wedding present, Fritz Frith gave the couple a carved tray made of solid copper and

Len's father, Fred Algernon
Beadell

Len's mother, Viola Pearl Beadell
(née Mackay)

a cutlery set in which each utensil was inscribed with the letter F. The copper tray remains a Beadell family heirloom.

After learning of the availability of some small farms in the Dural area near Hornsby, north of Sydney, the newlyweds soon took up residence at a property named Redhill. Their house was a typical cottage of the time. A large 'conservatory lounge-verandah' overlooked a deep valley which was covered with maiden-hair ferns and a sprinkling of waratahs. A small creek meandered across the valley floor. There were also excellent views beyond the valley to distant hills covered with virgin bushland. A citrus orchard (mainly oranges and mandarins) was established close to the house. Viola took great pride in caring for a beautiful country garden comprising roses, fuschias, nasturtiums and pink geraniums.

The Beadell's first child, daughter Phyllis, was born at Redhill on 31 December 1917.

The family left Redhill on 4 July 1921 and began an itinerant existence over the next decade. They initially lived at Mossman but, in early October 1922, relocated to a rural holding called The Glen in Taylor Street, Pennant Hills West, now a residential suburb

Len's sister, Phyllis

of Sydney. Fred managed The Glen for a Mr Harpham, who also shared the property's residence with the Beadells. There were 15 acres of mixed orchard to look after at The Glen, as well as over 1 000 chickens and numerous cows. Fred's generosity in shoeing neighbours' horses became well known. He would regularly come home after a full day's work in the orchard to find several draught horses tethered to his shed. He'd put his own horse away, set up the forge and anvil, shoe the horses and leave them tied up for the neighbours to collect the next morning. The neighbours would often say: 'Fred's a beaut bloke, he'd do anything for you except say gidday!'

The Glen, Pennant Hills West, where Len was born.

An early photograph of Len.

A son, Leonard Beadell, was born to the family at The Glen on 21 April 1923. Outback Australia would never be the same ...

On 22 March the following year, the family left The Glen and moved to Castle Hill west of Sydney, where they temporarily rented a brick house from a Mr Strang. In August 1924, they moved to another residence called Carona in Cecil Avenue, Castle Hill. This property featured beautifully manicured gardens and lawns as well as around two acres of cultivated land bearing mixed fruit trees. In March 1927 Len's father left his then current position as motor engineer with the local Shire Council to begin a career with a major oil company. The change in vocation meant that the Beadells, with some degree of sadness, had to leave their Castle Hill home. Len's mother wrote at the time: 'I think we have all had the happiest time imaginable here [at Carona] and I shall always remember it with affection.'

On 28 March 1927, they moved to a new residence called Aratoria in Curtis Street, Ryde, also west of Sydney.

Aratoria was a comfortable brick cottage, with every modern convenience – electric lights, gas stove, gas copper and electric iron.

From August to December 1928, Len became very ill and severely weakened. He spent most of August and November in hospital, during which time he had both his adenoids and tonsils removed. He also had a large growth on his neck, which was of great concern to his doctors.

L EN was back in hospital on 10 December to have an operation to excise the growth. He remained under close medical care until 28 December.

In Len's sister Phyllis's own words: 'It was a very worrying time for my parents and, given this debilitating period of Len's childhood, one could never believe that one day the tag of *Iron Man of the Inland* could be attributed to him. Yet our mother said when Len was still quite young: "That boy will make his mark in the world." And how right she was! As a child, Len's character remained similar to that of his later adult life – compassionate, unselfish, and with a cheerful, happy disposition.'

Len (far left, with ball) at the Beadell's Castle Hill home.

The Beadell Family Tree[a]

EDWIN BEADELL

1. Frank
   (Lived in Chicago)

2. Olive
   (Lived in London)

3. Ivy
   (Lived in Australia and cared for Len's grandparents)

MARIE BEADELL

4. FRED ALGERNON BEADELL
   b 17.9.1889
   d 28.7.1978

VIOLA PEARL MACKAY
b 18.10.1889
d 31.8.1949

1. PHYLLIS BEADELL
   b 31.12.1917

2. LEN BEADELL
   b 21.4.1923

ANNE MATTHEWS
b 19.5.1941

1. CONNIE SUE BEADELL
   b 11.12.1961

2. GARY BEADELL
   b 27.2.1963

Ann-Indra Anthony
b 7.7.1963

3. JACQUELINE BEADELL
   b 7.5.1965

Russell Asser
b 16.7.1965

1. JOSEPH LEONARD BEADELL
   b 10.7. 1996

1. Mitchell Asser
   b 31.1.1992

2. Courtney Asser
   b. 1.10.1994

Footnote[a]   Len's great grandparents were Frederick Beadell and Annie (née Pratt). According to Edwin Beadell's birth certificate, they lived at St John's Wood, Hampstead, Middlesex, England. Frederick Beadell's occupation was listed as artist in water colour.

END NOTES

The following extract on the wedding of Len's parents appeared in the local Townsville newspaper in 1914. The flowery language and quaint style of writing, so typical of this era, is priceless.

A PRETTY wedding was celebrated at St. James's Cathedral by the Ven. Archdeacon Crozier on 19th December, when Mr Fred A. Beadell, only son of Mr and Mrs Edwin Beadell, Woodlands, Mosman, Sydney, was united in the holy bonds of matrimony to Miss Viola Mackay, youngest daughter of Mr and Mrs Herbert Mackay, Townsville. The bride, who was given away by her eldest brother, Mr H.D. Mackay, wore a simple gown of ivory merveilleux with an overdress of embroidered chiffon voile, and a wide satin belt. She wore a charming pink glacé hat trimmed with small bunches of pink roses, and white heather. Her lovely shoulder bouquet, which was composed of stephanotis and bridal roses was entwined with pink tulle. She also wore a handsome brooch set with rubies, which, with the bouquet, were the gifts from the bridegroom. Miss Marjorie Humphry, who acted as bridesmaid, looked very dainty in a cream lace costume with touches of pink, cream satin sash; small hat en suite. She also carried a bouquet of pink roses, stephanotis, and maiden hair fern, with pink satin streamers, and wore a circlet brooch set with turquoises and pearls, both gifts of the bridegroom. Mr Alfred Mackay supported the bridegroom in the capacity of best man. The bride's present to the bridegroom was a pair of gold initialled sleeve links. Mrs Mackay's costume was a handsome black merveilleux, with black lace tunic relieved with white net and a tuscan straw hat with graceful drooping feathers. Miss Mackay, sister of the bride, wore a dress of white chiffon voile embroidered wedgewood blue, small white hat swathed with tulle, and bunches of tiny blue roses and forget-me-nots on brim. After the ceremony the guests were entertained at Mandalay, Melton Hill, where the usual toasts were honoured. The bride's travelling dress was a smart check coat and skirt, white silk turned down collar and cuffs, fancy buttons, panama hat en suite.

Mr and Mrs Beadell left by the Ayr train in the afternoon en route for Bowen, and were passengers by the Wyreema for Sydney. The honeymoon will be spent at Katoomba, Blue Mountains. Their future home will be Red Hill, Hornsby, Sydney.

Viola Beadell kept a diary for Len's sister Phyllis from 1918 to 1928, a period which incorporated Len's first five years of life. The following extracts relating to Len's childhood are taken from this diary, with permission of Phyllis. (The descriptions in this chapter of the various homes in which the Beadells lived are also taken from this diary).

21 April 1923: Today, God sent me a dear little baby brother and we are going to call him 'Leonard' after Uncle Frank Leonard who lives in America. He is a darling little boy and we all love him very much.

15 September 1923: We took Len down to Sydney to be christened at All Saints Church, Woollahra, by the Reverend Canon Langley.

7 October 1923: Len started to cut his first two teeth. He is six months old and weighs $17^{1}/_{2}$ lb, which is a pound and a half more than baby boys usually weigh at that age.

4 November 1923: Len sat up for the first time. A later entry also states that he started to walk before he reached 11 months.

31 December 1924: Len is growing into a lovely boy and just beginning to talk.

25 December 1925:   This is the second Christmas Day we have spent at Carona. [Len's] Dad made a lovely Christmas tree which was laden with presents for Len and myself [Phyllis] ... Len got a new teddy bear, mechanical dog and horse, a book, a trumpet, a drummer toy, also a ball besides a lucky stocking and a box of sweets. We all had a lovely Christmas dinner and ... Len was lucky in getting some silver pieces in his pudding.

21 April 1928:   Today is Len's birthday. He is now five years of age, and is such a sensible boy. We gave him a lovely party. Grandpa gave him a watch and chain, Grandma a football, Auntie Joy a large drawing slate, Daddy a pop gun, Mum a new pair of shoes and socks, and I [Phyllis] gave him some blocks. Edna and Jean also came to the party and gave him presents of handkerchiefs. Mum made a large three-storey birthday cake and put in five three-pence coins. Dad iced and decorated the cake with five candles. Len lit the candles and cut the cake and we also sang happy birthday to him. Afterwards we had a concert and played games until bed-time.

Chapter 2

SCHOOL, SCOUTS AND SURVEYING

L EN began his primary education at Gladesville Public School near Ryde, west of Sydney, in 1928. However, within two years his parents moved again, this time to a new house called St Clair in Eurella Street, Burwood, a suburb of Sydney.

The family remained at Burwood for the duration of Len's school years. Len completed the remainder of his primary education at Burwood Public School. He then attended Sydney Grammar School where his mother hoped he would 'get the rough edges knocked off him.'

Len stated: 'I wasn't any trouble at school and I wasn't a handful for the teachers, but I was a bit, well, unorthodox.'

At around seven years of age, Len befriended a schoolmate named Jimmy Owens, who later became a life-long companion. Jimmy was active in the local scouts (the 1st Burwood Scout Group). He encouraged Len to come along to a meeting. Len had no idea what scouts were about, but decided to accompany Jimmy anyway. He was introduced to the scoutmaster, John Richmond ... Len's life was changed forever.

John Richmond (also called Skip or Mr Mond by Len) served Australia in the First World War as a lieutenant in the Intelligence Corps. He was employed by the Metropolitan Water Sewerage and Drainage Board of Sydney as a draughtsman for five years and then as surveyor for the next 39 years. He became a Fellow of the Institute of Surveyors. Richmond was a bachelor who devoted his life to surveying and scouts. He owned a house, but lived in his backyard. He slept in a tent which was permanently erected in the yard. As one tent became too weatherbeaten to live in, he would replace it with another – the thought of sleeping inside was totally preposterous! He worked in his shed, or 'office' as he called it. Len fondly recalled that 'it was a real adventure

Len, the schoolboy

going into Skip's office.' It contained anvils, lathes, emery wheels, vice, spring balances, chains, an endless array of tools, a range of theodolites (some of which belonged to Richmond's father, William, who was also a surveyor), and a miscellany of home-made inventions such as calculators, topographical instruments and circular side drills. John Richmond was clearly very different to most people; yet like Len, he was admired and loved by almost everyone he met.

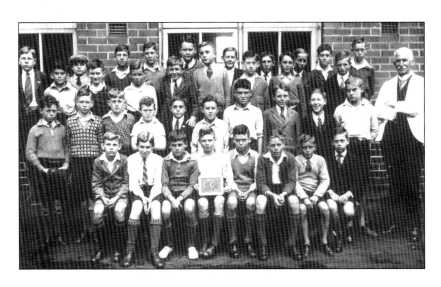

A photo taken at the Burwood Public School on 18 October 1935. Len, age 12, is pictured second from the left in the front row.

John Richmond (left), Len and Len's father, Fred Beadell.

Richmond's weekend survey trips, or 'treasure hunts' as he liked to call them, became legendary among the Sydney scouting fraternity. At each weekly scout meeting, he would select around half a dozen children and ask them whether they would like to come on a weekend excursion. Len became one of Richmond's keenest pupils and he recalled how 'Mr Mond saw I had a bit of potential and would somehow single me out to go every time.' Len would yearn for the weekend to come. He spent virtually every weekend from 1931 to 1941 (right through his school years) in the bush with Richmond.

The survey trips were conducted within a 150-kilometre radius of Sydney, mainly around Kiama and in the Blue Mountains. Richmond would pick up his willing helpers on Saturday morning in his bull-nosed Morris and return them home late on Sunday night. The children brought only a small back pack and a frypan. They loved camping in the bush, cooking (and burning) the porridge, trudging up and down hills carrying theodolites and other equipment, and searching for old survey markers, as if on a treasure hunt. There was, however, a purpose behind the excursions. Richmond was establishing a trigonometric network

*Len and the boys with
John Richmond's
Chevrolet Tourer,
equipped with
'trig' poles.*

for the water board and planning the location and pipeline connection between major dams supplying water to Sydney. All the weekend work was unpaid, but that was irrelevant to him. He simply loved surveying and he loved the bush. Around 1936, Richmond sold his Morris and paid £250 for a new 1936 Chevrolet Tourer. It had a soft rag roof but no windows. He made a tripod rack for the back bumper bar and fitted trigonometric poles along both sides of the vehicle, which meant the doors couldn't open. The only way into the car was to climb through an open window!

Forays to areas well beyond the Sydney environs were occasionally interspersed between the weekend excursions. For example, Richmond took scout groups (including Len) to Bathurst in New South Wales for a gold prospecting trip, and to Belair National Park near Adelaide for a national scout jamboree. A major highlight was a trip to Lord Howe Island during Christmas 1938.

Richmond had access to several early maps of Lord Howe Island. He decided to go to the Island and carry out a series of astronomical observations to determine whether the latitudes and longitudes plotted on the maps were correct. It was something to do at Christmas time – just for fun! Six lads, including Len, each paid £10 to accompany Richmond. They sailed from Sydney to the island aboard a small ship, the *Miranda*. Len spent an intensive two-week period working alongside Richmond. They took parallel star observations, with Len using Richmond's theodolite and Richmond using one of his father's instruments. It was a great learning experience for Len. Richmond gave Len expert instruction and would praise and encourage him at every opportunity. Astronomical observations were Richmond's great love and speciality; he had written a book on the subject. On their return to Sydney, Richmond and Len spent numerous nights calculating and reworking the data they had collected. Their conclusion was that Lord Howe Island was 10 kilometres out of position (by latitude) on the original map. Richmond's work colleagues at the water board constantly ribbed him thereafter saying 'when are you going to tow the island back to its original position?'

Len became totally engrossed in Richmond's work. He rode his bicycle to see Richmond on weeknights between excursions. The two spent countless hours in the 'office' where they quietly discussed star observations and Richmond explained the intricacies of theodolites – how they worked and how to use them correctly. The sessions would end around 11.30pm when Richmond would take out his watch and wind it up, indicating to Len it was time to return home. Richmond was also responsible for teaching Len the art of surveyor lettering, a skill in which Len excelled and took great pride. Len spent many hours laboriously practising his lettering technique and then showing his completed work to Richmond for critical appraisal. Richmond's influence in shaping Len's future career was profound. Quite simply, Len regarded John Richmond as his mentor. Len stated: 'He showed me that it was possible to enjoy all the pleasures of the bush (particularly camping), while at the same time still doing something useful and constructive (that is, surveying).'

Len's school work never suffered as a consequence of the Richmond factor, although Len did regard school as 'incidental' and his schoolmates regarded Len as 'different.' They would often say to him: 'When are you ever going to drop your act?' Len would reply: 'What act? This is just me.' In his last three years at Sydney Grammar, Len developed an interest in wrought ironwork. He fashioned a set of tuning forks from an old car axle and spring on his home forge and anvil. The forks were used widely in physics classes at the school. He also won the school's Carter Prize for creativity in designing and making a linked chain from a solid bar of iron.

The day after his final school exam in 1939, Len headed north on a train bound for Newcastle. He was met by John Richmond, who had been seconded from the Sydney water board to the Lands Department to carry out military mapping in northern New South Wales between Kempsey and Murwillumbah. World War II had just broken out and there was a flurry of activity to complete military mapping exercises in areas that were considered potentially vulnerable to attack by the Japanese. As part of this mapping exercise, Len and Richmond spent the next two months doing what they liked best – camping in the bush and making star observations. But there was one significant difference. Richmond had secured Len a temporary surveying position with the water board. Len recalled: 'I was straight from school and on the Sydney water board payroll. I couldn't believe my good fortune. I'd been surveying all my life just for fun, and now I was getting paid for it. I was used to walking up and down hills carrying theodolites but now, as I walked up a hill, I could think, I got ten bob for that hill!'

END NOTES

Camping Excursions With Mr Mond

The following extracts are taken from Len's personal Scout Diaries which, as a young lad, he assiduously kept from 1934 to 1937. They give an insight into the fun and adventure which Len had on his many camping/weekend excursions with John Richmond.

Wentworthville to Prospect, December 1934 (2 days)

We arrived at our camp spot at about 5 o'clock and, after pitching our tent and finishing our tea, we wrapped ourselves in our blankets and went over to the big camp fire. It was my first camp so I did not sleep but nearly dozed off once. Next morning after breakfast we had a good swim and, after a Scouts Own Service, we amused ourselves until dinner time. I nearly passed tracking.

Waterfall to Heathcote, 27 - 29 June 1936

Hiked from Waterfall to trig station Westmicot and then on to our camp. The ground was sloping and sandy, and near a river. We did not have a camp fire that night so we went straight to bed. It was very cold that night and we could not get warm at all. Being sandy ground, the sand got in our blankets and made us uncomfortable. So we had a very nasty night of it. Next morning after a swim, Mr Richmond was giving out packets of Steam Rollers and other kinds of lollies to the Scouts who found any kind of survey mark.

'A' Scouts Camp, 18 - 19 July 1936

On our first day we had to find a tree marked 'A' where we were to camp. When I found it (with much trouble) I put up a tent and prepared for dinner. I made a stew for my first class badge and passed it. That afternoon we had a billy-boiling competition and

I came 4th, getting 17 marks for our patrol. We had to get some sticks and a billy of water. Then Mr Mond measured out $^1/_2$ pint of water and poured the rest over our wood. Then we had to make a fire with our wet wood and boil the $^1/_2$ pint of water. Next morning I made some porridge, but as Mr Mond thought it tasted like 'Wall-nut' I did not pass. That day he took us around the bush until he lost us and then left us saying 'Find a certain tree marked with a white ring painted around it.' I was the first to find it so I went back to camp, had dinner and went home in Mr Mond's car.

Wentworth Falls to Burragorang Valley, 26 December 1936 -3 January 1937

Left from Wentworth Falls station on Boxing Day and hiked a fair way to the first camp spot. The weather was very fine the first day. That day's hiking was mostly downhill which made us very shaky and tired. The first camp spot was near the river in the middle of a big patch of bracken fern which had to be cut away before we could pitch our tents. Camped near the Cox River the second night in an open field. Next day we hiked until we reached Burragorang Valley. It rained heavily while we were hiking. Next morning for breakfast we were issued porridge and, being the second time I've ever cooked it, it all dried and stuck to the billy; but after that lesson I could cook it all right. As we were swimming and paddling in canoes the time passed until New Year's Eve when we had a big camp fire. I played my mouth organ and took part in a play at the camp fire.

Mt Victoria return via Kanimbla Valley, 26 - 29 March 1937

We hiked through dense ferns and down steep mountains. After the second day of hard hiking, we came to our camping spot. It was a fairly hard hike down but it was worth it because this spot was all grass and trees and there was a fair-sized running creek with crystal clear water about four or five yards away from my tent. That night we had a great big camp-fire, one of the biggest we have ever had. I played my mouth organ. The next day we hiked about two miles back to Cummins farm. Mr Richmond had to carry one of the boys all the way back while I carried his pack as well as my own.

The Theodolite – What is it and how does it work?

From the Macquarie Encyclopedic Dictionary ISBN 0 949757 56 X
theodolite, n. an instrument for measuring horizontal or vertical angles. [coined word; origin unknown]

E ARLY theodolites were just that! An instrument, with a sighting tube and sometimes a mounted telescope, built around a horizontal and a vertical axis, with readable scales for the measurement of horizontal angles (for direction) and vertical angles (for elevation and/or depression). These scales were read 'directly', that is, there were no magnification aids, which limited their accuracy. Later improvements saw magnification devices on the scales and, later still, the incorporation of verniers on the scales which greatly improved accuracy. All measurements were written into field books/notes, and used generally in the office for the calculation of distances/areas/volumes etc.

These early theodolite telescopes had an 'inverted image', that is, the image was back-to-front and upside-down to avoid the use of an additional lens element, which would have reduced the clarity of the viewed image. It was something that early surveyors had to get used to and, when 'right reading' telescopes/ instruments came onto the scene decades later, there were many older surveyors in the profession who still preferred to use the old instruments.

The introduction of etched glass scales, and microptic theodolites in the mid-30s was a boon to surveyors. No longer had one to interpret the silvered brass scales, which were prone to discolouration, and vernier readings. As a bonus they could be easily illuminated for night time or underground applications – a far cry from the primitive multiple candle illumination used on the early silvered verniers. Unfortunately we were still stuck with the inverted image. The theodolite used by Len Beadell for most of his work in the Army Survey Corps, in the Top End, and in the establishment of the Woomera Rocket Range and the Maralinga and Emu test sites was a UK-built, Cooke, Troughton & Simms microptic with $3^1/_2$ inch (approx 90mm) scales, which cost about £340.

Later developments, resulting from improved lens-making procedures involving coating compounds, allowed the introduction of the long sought-after additional lens component to allow 'right-reading' telescopes, which are now incorporated into all modern instruments. Measurements, and observed readings, were at this time still written into a field book for later interpretation in the office environment.

The early 1960s saw the introduction of piggy-back electronic distance measuring (EDM) systems, which were generally attached above the theodolite telescope axis and allowed measurements to be taken directly to a field-hand holding a prism reflector. This development gave the capability to observe and record both horizontal and vertical angles and distances in the field. Len, I am sure, would have given his right arm for one of these! Integrated EDM's were not far behind. Here the EDM was integrated into the telescope thus eliminating mechanical errors caused by the misalignment of telescope and EDM reference points.

Most modern-day instruments are what is commonly called 'digital', where all readings/data are displayed in numeric form and can be either recorded long-hand or, as it is in most cases nowadays, stored directly onto electronic field books for later downloading into a personal computer for data manipulation. More recent developments have seen the introduction of 'automatic target recognition' theodolites!

Where it will all end is anybody's guess. What once took Len, and others like him, a whole night to 'fix' their position from the stars, followed by several hour's calculation, can now be achieved in a matter of minutes by using the most basic of Global Positioning System, (GPS), receivers!

John D A Harrison
BM, BEM, FIEMS (Aust)

Len and his trusted theodolite

Copy of a short reference which John Richmond wrote for Len on 25 January 1949.

I have known Leonard Beadell for the past 17 years as a member of the Burwood Scout Troop.

He has always proved himself a true scout in the finest sense of the word. His zeal for duty is clearly shown by his splendid record of war service.

He has been associated with me for many years during my work on the trig. survey and I can not speak too highly of his enthusiasm, helpfulness and resourcefulness upon all occasions.

John Richmond
Surveyor

Chapter 3

$\mathcal{A}$ CALL TO DUTY

T HE year was 1941 and Len was 18. He received a letter in the mail which stated: 'Bring two cut lunches, report to the army recruiting office, be prepared to enlist in the army for the duration of the war and 12 months thereafter.' A number of Len's scouting friends of similar age received their conscription letters at about the same time. All were keen to enlist. In this era of Australia's history, it was considered cowardly not to defend your country. Len often related the following story: 'A young man dressed in civilian clothes was sitting on an electric train bound for Sydney. An elderly lady walked up to the man, stared at him, and dropped a white feather in his lap. This was the ultimate insult to a young man at the time, as it signified he was a coward. The man stood up, called out loudly to the packed carriage and said: 'This lady has just given me a present, a white feather!' He then pulled up his trousers to reveal an aluminium leg. He continued: 'I had my leg blown off in the Middle East six months ago and was medically discharged from the army. And this lady has just given me a white feather.' The lady's face went scarlet with embarrassment, but this true story poignantly illustrates the level of patriotism expected and demanded by the Australian community at the time.'

Len was initially drafted to the Army Service Corps at Bathurst. He spent most of his time behind the wheel of three-ton trucks transporting troops, ammunition and food supplies. In February 1942, Len was called before his Commanding Officer and informed that he was being transferred to the 2nd Australian Field Survey Company AIF (which was part of the Royal Australian Survey Corps). Len couldn't believe his luck. He was stationed at Strathfield Army Headquarters near his hometown Burwood. He was able to continue his work as a surveyor; and he knew

Len, the young soldier.

every senior officer in the Survey Corps because they had all been friends or acquaintances of John Richmond. As Len related: 'I had my brand new army uniform on, hat turned up at the sides and chinstrap tight, and I had to salute blokes I'd known all my life! But that was the army way; you saluted the rank not the person.'

Len's first assignment with the Survey Corps was to undertake a 50-kilometre pack-horse trip into mountainous terrain west of Sydney to carry out trigonometric survey work. Lieutenant Noel Fletcher was in charge of the small party of men chosen for the trip. Fletcher developed a long-standing friendship with Len and later became surveyor general of New South Wales. Prior to departing on their journey, all the pack horses needed shoeing. Len readily volunteered for the task, provided that he was allowed to wear his old hob-nailed boots and not the 'slippers' which the army issued. The party took four days to reach the top of the mountains. The horses were laden with heavy equipment and bags of flour, and the climb was slow and difficult. They stayed in the mountains for two weeks, cutting down large trees that were two axe-handles thick and clearing an 800-metre path between the scrub. It was back-breaking work, but nothing unusual for Len who had spent most of his youth doing similar chores for John Richmond. Towards the end of the exercise, Len was involved in an accident in which a felled tree knocked him to the ground and pinned his legs. He was forced to endure an agonising horse ride down the hill through thick scrub to safety. Len stated: 'But I didn't mind, I thought army life was great, all beaut stuff you know.'

After recovering from this accident, Len was asked to join an army survey party who were carrying out military mapping at Murwillumbah. Len knew this area well as he had worked there with John Richmond immediately after leaving school. Several weeks were spent in difficult terrain preparing contour maps for Army Headquarters. Remarkably, some of the instruments the army were using had been designed by John Richmond.

On 26 October 1942 Len and ten of his colleagues were sent to New Guinea aboard the *SS Tarcoona* to serve in the 8th Field Survey Section AIF (also known as the New Guinea Survey Section). Len spent the next 14 months of his life machetteing through dense tropical jungle in the Owen Stanley Ranges, wading knee-deep through mud and mosquito-infested swamps, and enduring constant tropical downpours while, at the same time, attempting to undertake surveys and perform operational mapping. It was impossible to remain dry as the soldiers had nothing but the clothes they stood in. Len contracted recurrent episodes of malaria (a disease which continued to plague him in later life), dengue fever and scabies; the latter infection attacked his wrists, knees, elbows and ankles. Len described his battle with scabies thus: 'The little mites would bury themselves a half-inch under my skin, lay their eggs, die and then erupt into little craters all over me.' But, in the face of these hardships, he never lost his indomitable spirit: 'It might have been hard, but it sure beat Shakespeare or algebra.'

Len developed a great affection for the indigenous Papua New Guinean people, describing them as 'golden treasures.' Their courage and endurance was remarkable. They helped the Australian soldiers carry heavy equipment on wooden planks

Members of the Eighth Field Survey Section, Port Moresby, 1942.
Len is kneeling, front row, far right.

through the most difficult terrain; often their reward was to share
a meal of rice, bully beef and dog biscuits with the soldiers. Len
recalled an occasion when one native almost completely severed
his hand on an open can of bully beef. Len helped bandage the
wound temporarily while one of the man's companions walked
day and night for four days to reach the coast and bring back help
to his injured friend.

During another survey field trip, Len set up camp for the night
in dense jungle and lay down to sleep. He felt an excruciating
bite in his left shoulder, presumably from a spider. The whole left
side of his body was paralysed when he awoke next morning. He
spent two weeks in an army hospital unable to move his arm.
When he had almost recovered, a tragic accident occurred near
the hospital. A Liberator aeroplane, bound for Port Moresby and
full of soldiers, was taking off from a nearby runway. A line of
army trucks carrying other soldiers to the Kokoda Trail waited
near the end of the runway. The plane exploded on takeoff and
careered into the line of trucks. There were many fatalities, while
numerous soldiers were severely injured. Len later sat in his

hospital bed watching a fellow soldier dangling the stump of his arm in a basin of salt. He reflected soberly on the insignificant nature of the pain he had suffered as a result of the spider bite.

It was during one of Len's sojourns to the edge of the Kokoda Trail that he first saw a four-wheel-drive jeep. Len was astonished by its capacity to 'go anywhere' and immediately wrote to John Richmond about the vehicle. At the time, he had little idea that this mode of transport would later become so much a part of his working life.

Len spent most of 1943 conducting surveys of the coastal area around Milne Bay. During one excursion his small boat broke down and his party was stranded for a three-week period. They lived on wild pigs, coconuts and pumpkins, which they 'borrowed' from the nearby gardens of local indigenous people.

Len befriended a group of army artists who were stationed at the base camp near Milne Bay. The artists had a crucial role in converting information given to them by the survey team into map form. Doug Albion (who later became an art editor for *Reader's Digest*) and Lionel Taprell (whom Len described as the best pencil portrait artist he had ever seen) took Len under their wing, encouraged him, and nurtured his artistic talent. Len developed a particular skill for cartoon-style sketches with humorous overtones; that is 'sketches that would immediately make people laugh.' He retained this skill for the rest of his life. Later in his army career, Len renewed acquaintance with another artist, Norman Hetherington. He had been one of Len's boyhood idols and was part of John Richmond's scouting fraternity. Hetherington later worked as an artist for the Sydney *Bulletin* for 18 years and developed the character of Mr Squiggle for the television series of the same name.

In December 1943 Len was sent back to Australia to take a well-earned rest from the rigours of the New Guinea jungle. He was assigned to the 6th Australian Army Survey Topographical Company and worked for short periods in Brisbane, Katoomba, Townsville, Marryatville and Toowoomba. However, he headed back to Lae, New Guinea, aboard the *SS Katoomba* on 29 March 1945 as a member of the 3rd Field Survey Company.

Some of Len's earliest sketches.

Len was part of a team which was sent by ship from Lae to Wewak on the northern coast of New Guinea. The ship was in derelict condition and the living conditions were appalling. The men slept on rusty iron floors in the vessel's hull. The stench of rotten coconut husks pervaded the entire living quarters. Tropical rainstorms poured through gaping holes in the ship's deck, saturating the soldiers' clothing and equipment. One tin of bully beef was shared between three men. There were no toilets. Len suffered violently from episodes of seasickness.

When they arrived at Wewak, the surrounding jungle was alive with Japanese soldiers. Their camp here was rudimentary. Banana leaves strung between tree branches provided the only shelter from the torrential rain. Fallen coconuts from a nearby plantation formed their staple diet. Their only source of drinking water was from rainfall which collected in large depressions made by navy shelling. Sentries were regularly posted around these waterholes. Len recalled one particular night when three sentries were killed while guarding the waterholes. During that night the sky was repeatedly lit up by flashes of lightning. As one flash occurred, three shots were fired from Japanese soldiers hiding in the nearby jungle. When the next flash lit up the night, the sentries lay dead in the waterhole.

The purpose of sending Len and his fellow troopers to Wewak was two-fold. First, the survey team was endeavouring to map as much of the nearby coast as possible. There were fears the Japanese could reclaim part of the coast from the allied forces. It was critical for the allies to gain as much knowledge as possible about the coast to ensure assault missions and artillery firing ranges could be planned and calculated appropriately. No previous field work had ever been carried out in the region and the army was totally reliant on star observations carried out by Len and his colleagues. Secondly, a new airstrip needed to be built at Wewak to replace the former runway which had been destroyed by artillery shelling. The airstrip was duly completed in August 1945 and Len undertook his first-ever plane flight in a Dakota DC-3 from Wewak to Maprik, about an hour away.

On arrival at Maprik, Len was greeted by a number of jubilant officers who stated that the war was over. He recalled: 'I thought, oh sure, the war's over; I've been hearing that for years!' But the buoyant mood of the troops at Maprik slowly made him realise that the officers were not teasing and, yes, the war was truly over. Len felt mixed emotions. To him personally, the impact of the news was minimal. In many ways he had enjoyed the war years. He had experienced a series of adventures and, throughout his time in the army, he had been doing what he loved most – surveying. He was still young; he had no family commitments; and he remained a free spirit. But for his colleagues, he felt relief and compassion. Many were in their forties and had left behind their wives and children for up to six wasted years.

Len and several companions spent the next few days prospecting for gold in a nearby creek. They used army frypans as panning equipment. According to Len, one of his mates found a number of sizeable pieces of gold. He melted the gold down, poured it over his work spanner, and then covered the spanner with grease. He took the gold-coated spanner back to Australia in his tool box.

A Dakota DC-3 was due to arrive in Maprik to take the soldiers back to Wewak and eventually home to Australia. However, as it touched down on the sodden airstrip, the plane skidded sideways and came to an abrupt halt. One of the plane's wings was buried in mud and a propeller was damaged beyond repair. Several days later another plane arrived, this time without incident. Len was flown to Wewak and then Lae, where he boarded a troop ship bound for Brisbane. On the trip home, Len regularly entertained the troops with some impromptu, light-hearted lectures on the joys of surveying. Len's spirit remained high as he sailed home to Australia.

END NOTES

Well-known Sydney artist, Norman Hetherington, discusses his association with Len and comments on Len's unique style of sketching.

L EN and I both grew up in the Sydney suburb of Burwood. A Boy Scout concert was being organised and I (although not a Scout) was dragooned into doing a Lightning Sketch act to fill out the programme. This act included some caricature sketches of well-known members of the audience. Well, the undisputed hit of the act was the sketch of Len, who was not only a keen Scout, but quite a colourful character even then.

I had started contributing freelance cartoons to the *Bulletin*, so we got along famously. Len had his own style of drawing in black and white, quite wonderfully unique, with a completely self-taught quality. Any academic tuition would have ruined it. It also went beautifully with his writing style. He obviously had great fun both drawing and writing, and this enjoyment came across.

After the war, Len moved to work at Woomera and I stayed in Sydney. I'd been offered a job as a staff cartoonist on the *Bulletin* – which of course I jumped at. But we kept in touch. Each year, around Christmas, Len turned up, having driven across to Sydney from Woomera practically non-stop. You knew it was Len coming by his huge infectious laugh. He always brought a whole new batch of sketches with him – some to illustrate yet another book, and others for next year's Christmas card for the Long Range

Weapons Establishment. He was always seeking helpful advice and comments. Len was keen to learn and to improve. He would listen intently to all suggestions and then proceed to ignore them completely.

However, there was one suggestion of mine that I noticed he did include regularly in his drawings – the addition of a small lizard, usually on the sidelines, but always showing great interest in the proceedings.

One of the first drawings of Len's 'lizard friend'. This lizard subsequently became a regular feature of all Len's bush illustrations.

Kevin Whisson served with Len (or more specifically NX134865 Sgt Beadell) during the War from 1944 to 1945. He comments on Len's character and his unique 'dress sense' during this period. Kevin remained a long-time friend of Len's post-war and is the godfather of Len's daughter, Connie.

LEN was a man of very strong character, whose views on smoking and drinking were opposed by the majority of his fellow soldiers. His personal integrity allowed him to resist peer pressures and remain true to his principles during his army days and indeed throughout his entire life.

This integrity, coupled with bush skills learned as a youth, a wry understated sense of humour and a cheerfulness in adversity, made him a good bloke to have at your side; one on whom you could always rely.

Len was a very resourceful person able to put his hand to almost anything and always willing to pass his knowledge on to anyone interested. Not that he was the perfect soldier by any means – for he must have been the worst dressed man in the army

A sketch which Len drew for the occasion of Kevin Whisson's 60th birthday.

bar none! His 'working dress' would turn any 'spit and polish' Sar'
Major into a babbling epileptic.

A new kit of clothes would undergo the following transforma-
tion under Len's hands.

Boots: His hobs, as he called them, were fitted with additional
metal studs until the soles looked like the treads on a
Sherman tank.

Socks: Len hated wearing socks but, as a concession to
regulations, he would cut off the bottoms, just leaving
the leg portion sticking out above his boots.

Belt: Adopted his own leather belt, complete with pouches
for his pocket knife and whet stone.

Shirt: The sleeves were hacked off at the shoulders using the
above pocket knife, buttons removed and the whole
shirt worn outside his shorts.

Hat: Don't think he ever wore one!

Len was a man of unique personality and a good mate.

Chapter 4

TERRITORY TALES

ON returning to Australia, all army personnel were required to complete a further 12 months service before being discharged. Len was sent to the Darling Downs in Queensland where he carried out astronomical observations and general survey work for a series of new maps which the army was preparing. During the course of this work, he suffered a severe recurrence of malaria and required hospitalisation at Dalby. As Len left hospital, two officers from Brisbane drove up in a jeep and stopped him. They took Len aside and told him he had been hand-picked by Major Bill Johnson in Brisbane for a new and challenging task. (Major Johnson had been with Len on the ship which returned soldiers from Lae to Brisbane at the end of the war). A group of Canberra scientists from the CSIR (Council for Scientific and Industrial Research, later to be renamed CSIRO) were about to conduct a major scientific survey of the Darwin-Katherine region in the Northern Territory, with the aim of assessing the agricultural and pastoral potential of the area. They had asked the army to nominate a competent surveyor to accompany the expedition. Major Johnson had selected Len for the job. When asked whether he would be prepared to waive his discharge from the army for a further year and accept the position with the CSIR, Len said he 'thought about his decision for about one and a quarter seconds and said yes, too right, oh yes!'

Len spent the next two weeks completing some important triangulation work in the Darling Downs before heading off to Brisbane. He then travelled to Adelaide via Sydney (where he spent some time with his parents) and Melbourne (where he collected surveying equipment needed for the expedition). He soon boarded the Ghan train bound for Alice Springs, where he was to meet the CSIR expedition members. Len was about to encounter life in the Outback (or Wild West, as he called it) for the first time.

Two shearer's gangs, comprising about 30 men in total, were picked up by the train at Port Augusta. They were all completely drunk and spent the next day fighting and brawling amongst themselves, while Len desperately attempted to protect his valuable surveying equipment from being trampled or damaged. The intoxicated contingent were later unceremoniously thrown off the train at Oodnadatta.

Len alighted the train in Alice Springs on 8 June 1946. He was greeted by chief scientist and expedition leader, Dr Chris Christian, and other members of the party including geologist Bill Noakes, botanist Stan Blake and soil surveyor Alan Stewart.

Len's first day in Alice Springs proved eventful. He checked into the Underdowns Hotel, which provided large bungalow-style accommodation and was regarded as *the* place to stay in Alice Springs at the time. He then went for a leisurely walk around the town. Len was suddenly confronted by a large drunken man who was beating his wife. He stood between the distressed woman

Courtesy, CSIRO

The CSIRO survey party from left to right: Hugh Mason, Reg Munyard, Alan Stewart, Tom Howe, Roy Greenwood, Dr Chris Christian (sitting in truck), Stan Blake, Boram Mason and Len Beadell (no shoes!).

and the man. Len eventually calmed the man but was beginning to have second thoughts about life in the Wild West. Later that evening, he visited the father of one of his ex-army friends, Colin van Senden. Colin had told Len that, if he ever visited the Alice, he could find his father at Box 1, Alice Springs. They discussed the war years until around midnight when Len returned to Underdowns. The CSIR scientists had waited up for him. They were unsure where Len had been since checking in at Underdowns and had called the police who were looking all over town for him.

Within a few days, the expedition left Alice Springs. They drove north along the Stuart Highway in a 3-ton Blitz truck, a Chevrolet panel van and several jeeps, which were all ex-army vehicles. At Tennant Creek, they stopped at the local police station. The officer-in-charge was sitting on the front verandah with a revolver in his lap. He explained that he had jailed a man for drunken behaviour earlier in the day and he was waiting for the rest of his mates to come and attack the station!

The party continued on to Katherine, which at the time was a small town comprising a hotel, a homestead, several buildings and a CSIR experimental station. Dr Christian, who was an agricultural scientist, was growing several crops at the station. Len took time to visit Katherine Gorge during their short stopover. He drove the old Blitz truck on a narrow track out to the gorge. It was a pristine location in those days; the scenery was spectacular, the atmosphere was tranquil, and the water was crystal clear. Len had taken several drums with him and filled them with water for the local drink factory.

For the next four and a half months (from late June to early November 1946), the expedition focussed their scientific studies in an area bordered by Darwin, the Daly River, Katherine and the East Alligator River. Much of this land is now within the internationally-renowned Kakadu and Litchfield National Parks. Len's role was to fix the exact ground location of important topographical features and landmarks throughout the survey area by astronomical observation. This data, in combination with aerial photography and scientific information gathered by field traverses, was used to prepare a series of new maps showing the region's land systems, geomorphological units, and geology.

The working conditions encountered by the survey team were difficult. The mid-day sun was oppressive, mosquitoes were present in their billions, and much of the terrain was muddy and buffalo-trodden. Len's standard attire was no shirt, baggy shorts and bare feet. He explained: 'I wore no shoes or boots for most of that year; I was constantly walking in and out of ankle-deep mud in boggy ground. I quickly grew tired of trying to clean the mud off my boots at night. It was easier to wear no shoes at all. The soles of my feet became so hard that you could strike a wax match on them. At nearby Tipperary Station, one of the station-hands and I used to put on a bit of an act for the local children. He'd say that he wanted a cigarette. I'd put my right foot across my left knee, point the sole of my foot towards him, and he'd strike a match on my foot.'

The sodden terrain caused many problems for the expedition, with the Blitz truck proving particularly difficult to manœuvre through this country. On one occasion Len was driving the Blitz alone on the edge of the West Alligator River floodplain. The dry mud gave way and the truck sank down to its mudguard. Len had to walk 30 kilometres back to a buffalo shooter's camp to seek help. His arrival at 3am was not well received, but the shooters later obliged by helping Len dislodge the stranded vehicle.

While the expedition lived well on a regular diet of fresh bar-

*Len's vehicle,
bogged in the
West Alligator River
floodplain.*

ramundi and the occasional bush turkey, there were other hazards which required their close attention. Salt-water crocodiles abounded in the waterways. Len recalled one night when he was awakened by the scraping sound of an object brushing against the wooden leg of his camp stretcher. He leaned over to see a three-metre crocodile making its way through their camp. Thereafter, Len kept a loaded revolver tucked under his pillow. The country was also alive with wild buffalo. Whenever Len was alone in the bush at night carrying out star observations, he always carried a .303 rifle with him.

Len's spirit remained unfazed, despite the apparent hardships. He stated: 'After New Guinea, this work was easy! I loved every minute of my year in the Territory. There were new things happening every day; there were opportunities to see a bit of station life; and I met a number of real bush characters.' Len particularly enjoyed buffalo hunting with a group of professional shooters near Ben Ban Spring on Farrar's Station, south-east of Adelaide River. The buffaloes were killed for their hides, which were up to two centimetres thick. Once a buffalo was shot, a number of Aboriginal hands would skin the animal on site using large curved knives. The skin would eventually be laid flat on the ground and then folded slowly, one section at a time. The buffalo hides were sold mainly for their use as machine belts in local and interstate

Len buffalo shooting with 'King' and 'Jacky', near Ben Ban Spring.

factories. Len also regularly helped the young children milk the goats at the station. He stated: 'The children would come and wake me up and we'd milk 45 goats. I think we'd get about half a billy of milk out of all these goats! And all the time I was milking, the station's tame brolga would be pecking at my head with its long beak.'

Len made several round trips between base camps in the bush, Katherine, the Adelaide River and Darwin during the course of the year. Darwin was very much a frontier town, but showed the battle scars of Japanese bombing. The surveyor general of Darwin became very interested in Len's astronomical work and the two had numerous meetings regarding the expedition's progress. The drive along the Stuart Highway between Darwin and Katherine proved a constant source of entertainment for Len. On one occasion he stopped to give a lift to an old gentleman. In the course of general conversation, Len asked the man whether he'd ever been down south. The man nodded his head. Len asked: 'How far south?' 'Cairns' was the laconic reply. During another trip from Darwin to Katherine, Len noticed a large semi-trailer with a broken differential on the side of the road. He stopped to offer assistance. The driver stated that everything was fine and a new differential was on the way. Two weeks later on his return to Darwin, Len was surprised to see the damaged truck still in the same location with the driver standing nearby. Len said: 'Oh, you're still here, are you?' The driver replied: 'Yeah, no problem; I've only been waiting three months!'

It was during a stopover in Katherine that Len first encountered one of the Territory's true bush identities, 34-stone (216 kg) banana grower Tony Swanson. Len recalled: 'One day a bloke drove into our base camp at Katherine. He got out of his truck ... and he got out ... and he got out ... he just kept coming – all 34-stone of him. Each of his arms was thicker than my body. He drove the truck by sitting alongside the steering wheel – he could-n't sit behind it! I couldn't take my eyes off him. He asked me if I had any treacle. I hunted around and found some honey, which he said would do the trick. He then waddled over to the truck, started the engine, lifted the bonnet and poured the honey over

Tony Swanson at Marinboy, 1946.

the fan belt, which was slipping. I stood alongside him and the honey sprayed off the fan belt and went all over me. Tony burst into laughter, with one hand on the truck. As he was laughing, the whole truck was rocking up and down – and he only had one hand on it! As he drove away, several of the scientists from the CSIR came up to me and said that I had just met the number one identity in the Territory.'

The wet season duly arrived in late October, signalling the end of the expedition and curtailing one of the most enjoyable years of Len's life. The party headed south in early November via the Darling Downs, to Sydney and Canberra. Much to the chagrin of his superior officers, Len borrowed an army utility from Duntroon to carry his survey equipment back to its Melbourne base. On arrival in Melbourne, he was once again asked to stay on for another year in the army and to undertake another project. The biggest chapter of Len's life was about to unfold...

END NOTES

A formal scientific report on the 1946 CSIR expedition was written by Chris Christian and Alan Stewart, in collaboration with Lyn Noakes and Stan Blake, following their return to Canberra. The report was entitled Survey of Katherine-Darwin Region, 1946 Land Research Series No. 1. Commonwealth Scientific and Industrial Research Organisation, Australia, Melbourne 1952. The following selected information has been extracted from the report to provide a brief overview of the purpose and scope of the expedition.

General Report on Survey of Katherine-Darwin Region, 1946

Introduction

AN area of nearly 27 000 square miles in the Katherine-Darwin section of the Darwin and Gulf Land Administration Division of the Northern Territory was surveyed during the dry season of 1946.

The survey party was organised by the CSIR and included personnel from several cooperating bodies, including the Army Survey Corps. The full party comprised:

Officer-in-Charge	C.S. Christian	CSIR
Soils Officer	G.A. Stewart	CSIR
Geologist	L.C. Noakes	Commonwealth Bureau of Mineral Resources
Botanist	S.T. Blake	Department of Agriculture and Stock, Queensland
Transport and Supply Officer	H. Mason	
Mechanic	A.R. Greenwood	
Cook	F. Bradford	
	(subsequently replaced by T. Howe)	
Camp Assistant	R. Munyard	
Astro-Survey Personnel	Sgt. L. Beadell	Army Survey Corps
	Cpl. F. Cohen	

Area Surveyed

The area surveyed lies in the northernmost section of the Northern Territory (*figure 1*). The survey was confined to the region enclosed by the Daly and East Alligator River watersheds. This represents the north-west third of the Darwin and Gulf Land Administration District of the Northern Territory. This region includes the townships of Darwin, Katherine and Pine Creek; the Daly River settlement; Pine Creek and Finniss River; other mineral fields and several of the farms established by the Army for vegetable production. Although most of the area has been traversed

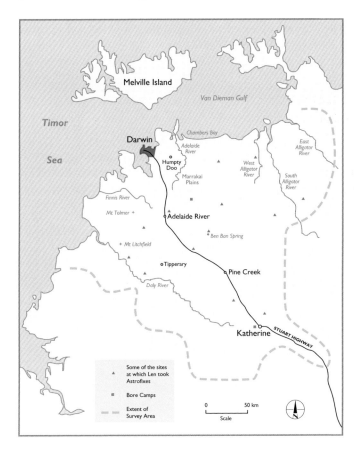

figure 1

at some time or other by prospectors, cattlemen, police, or members of the armed forces, little exact recorded information is available concerning much of this country.

Itinerary

The party left Melbourne on June 2, 1946, travelled by road to Quorn, S.A., by rail to Alice Springs, N.T., and then by road to Katherine, N.T., which was reached on June 15. The period June 15 to 23 was spent in final preparations for field work, which was commenced on June 24. The party remained in the field until the end of October when the approach of the wet season caused operations to cease. The return journey was begun early in November, the party travelling by road to Canberra, which was reached on November 15. An advance report on the survey was distributed in July 1947, and a full report published in 1952.

Scope and Objectives of Survey

The survey was conducted by land traverses that totalled over 3 000 miles and a brief aerial reconnaissance of about 800 miles.

The objectives of the survey were to record accurately the nature of the country, to assess its agricultural and pastoral potentialities and to make recommendations with respect to its development.

The region surveyed was examined mainly with respect to geology, geomorphology, topography, soils, vegetation, and present land use. In order that the developmental possibilities of the region might be assessed in a systematic way, the lands of the region were classified into land systems (defined as an area, or group of areas, throughout which can be recognised a recurring pattern of topography, soils, and vegetation). Eighteen land systems were described, mapped, their areas estimated and the pastoral and agricultural potentialities of each assessed.

The survey also had other responsibilities. It was scientific in nature and it was essential that the results of the survey should establish a foundation on which future more detailed work or special scientific investigations might be based. The following scientific reports/papers on the region's geology and flora were subsequently published:

1. LC Noakes. *A geological reconnaissance of the Katherine-Darwin Region, Northern Territory.* Bulletin No 16. *Commonwealth Bureau of Mineral Resources, Geology and Geophysics.*
2. ST Blake. *Botanical contributions of the Northern Australia Regional Survey. I. Studies of northern Australian Species of Eucalyptus. Australian Journal of Botany 1 (2): 185.*

Outcome of Survey

As a result of the survey, specific areas were identified in which future agricultural and pastoral development was considered most feasible and a general plan for the development of land industries of the region was subsequently formulated.

– o –

Reg Munyard, currently living near Canberra, was the expedition's Camp Assistant. Reg is now the sole surviving member of the expedition. He provides the following recollections of Len:

LEN joined our survey from the Army and spent a lot of the time out bush doing his astrofix work. He would return to the base camp to replenish his food and water and was then off again. He was a great bloke; there was always plenty of fun and laughter while he was around. He never smoked, drank, or used bad language. He very rarely wore boots in those days and, when he did, there would be no socks.

He regularly used the word awkward to refer to things he disliked. For example cigarettes were awkward sticks or awkward cylinders of wickedness. Alcoholic drink was awkward stuff that made you feel awkward. But one thing about Len – he was never *awkward.*

On the occasion of Dr Christian's 80th birthday in December 1987, Len was asked to contribute a short letter concerning his association with the scientist.

He wrote:

Memories of Dr Chris Christian

I FIRST met up with Chris in Alice Springs in April 1946, as a result of a request to our Army Survey Corps from the then CSIR just after World War II to make a surveyor available to travel with an impending Scientific Expedition to the Northern Territory. The requirement was somebody capable of astrofixing and I was chosen.

We spent the rest of 1946 together while Chris, his geologist Lyn Noakes, botanist Stan (Basher) Blake, and soil surveyor Alan Stewart carried out their relative studies. I ground-controlled by star observations the air photos on which all of their discoveries were recorded, in order that maps could be produced depicting their scientific findings.

Chris wore his Western light meter ragged, photographing everything in sight. I had been elated at the privilege of accompanying this exciting first combined Scientific Expedition into the Alligator River Country of Arnhem Land and it had taken me one second to accept the offer. It eventuated that this extra year as a member of the Survey Corps enabled me to be selected for a project which was to occupy the succeeding 41 years of my working life.

If it hadn't been for Chris and his 1946 expedition I would have accepted my normal army discharge and the future shape of things to come in Central Australia would have been completely different.

Thanks Chris for a wonderful year.

The very best memories and warmest regards.

Len Beadell B.E.M.

Chapter 5

$\mathcal{P}$IECING TOGETHER THE JIGSAW

L EN BEADELL has often been referred to as 'the last true Australian explorer.' He is best-known and best-remembered for his surveying and road-building exploits in the remote deserts of outback Australia between 1947 and 1963. Throughout this period, he worked as a Range Reconnaissance Officer for the Long Range Weapons Establishment (LRWE), Salisbury, South Australia. [The LRWE was later renamed the Weapons Research Establishment (WRE) and more recently became the Defence Science and Technology Organisation (DSTO)]. He was responsible for selecting sites for the Woomera Rocket Range and the British Nuclear Testing Programme (Emu and Maralinga). With his dedicated team of fellow workers, who have become immortalised in Australian folklore as the Gunbarrel Road Construction Party, Len also surveyed and constructed a network of outback roads spanning over 6 000 kilometres in length. These roads opened up, for the first time, over 2.5 million square kilometres of the Great Victoria, Great Sandy, Little Sandy and Gibson Deserts, the so-called Western Desert country of outback Australia. In building these roads, Len would initially undertake a solo reconnaissance of up to several hundred kilometres to survey the virgin country ahead and establish the most suitable course. He would then return to the construction party's base and lead the road-making team through the surveyed area. Len's courage in venturing alone into unknown wilderness where many of his predecessors had perished, and his unyielding commitment to his surveying work in the face of such brutally harsh conditions, remain unrivalled in modern-day Australian history.

The story of Len's work has already been vividly and humorously detailed in six best-selling books which he authored (see Chapter

9). As undoubtedly many readers will have already read and enjoyed Len's books, the aim of the following three chapters of his biography is to explore this hallmark period of Len's life in a different way to his own writings.

In this chapter, a brief summary of the main events and activities which took place in Len's life from 1946 to 1963 is presented in chronological sequence (with dates and times being sourced from Len's own meticulous personal diaries); the order in which such events occurred is not readily apparent from reading Len's books and has been a source of mystery for many of his dedicated followers.

1946

- The British and Australian governments agreed to establish a rocket range on mainland Australia. An area of land 1 600 kilometres long by 300 kilometres wide was needed for the rocket range.

- Colonel Fitzgerald, Director of the Australian Army Survey Corps, sought Len's interest in the project. Len was appointed to the task of finding an appropriate area for the range, following an interview with General Sir John Evetts from the British Army.

1947

- In March, Len selected a site just under 500 kilometres north of Adelaide which he felt was suitable for a rocket launching pad and a future township (soon to be named Woomera). He also chose the flight path for rockets to be fired from the site. The flight path extended north-west from Woomera, across the Great Victoria, Gibson and Great Sandy Deserts, to a point on the Eighty Mile Beach between Port Hedland and Broome in Western Australia.

- On 8 April, General Sir John Evetts and a party of seven (including Major Wynne-Williams) visited Len at the site. The name *Woomera* was first suggested for the location by Major Wynne-Williams. (Woomera is an Aboriginal term for a spear thrower, and refers to a wooden object used to launch a hunting spear).

1948

- Len continued the surveying of Woomera, and mapped the area to the north.

- It was initially intended that tracking instrumentation would be placed along the centreline of rocket fire, at predetermined distances from the rocket launching pad. Len conducted preliminary surveys of the area north-west of the centreline to Mt Eba.

Woomera was named after the Aboriginal term for a spear thrower.

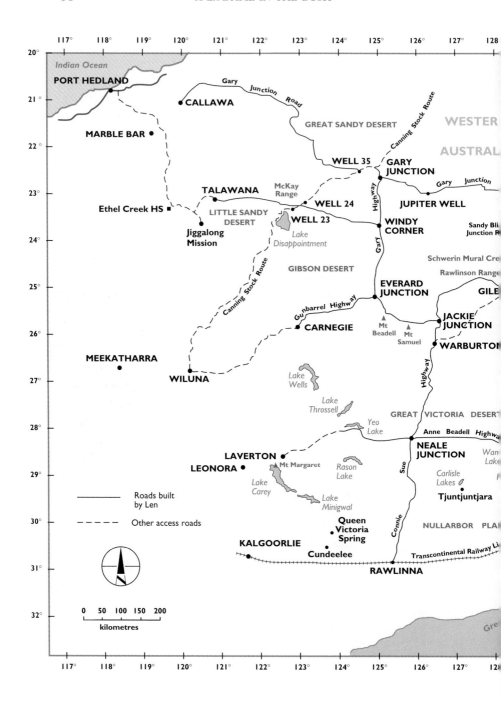

The Len Beadell outback road network

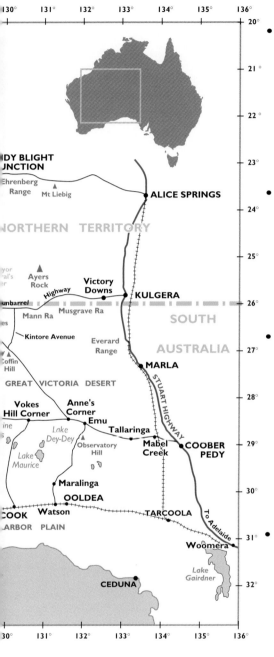

- Len received his official discharge papers from the army on 30 October. The papers stated his discharge was effective from 14 December 1948, after 2 552 days of service.

- On 2 November, he found an Aboriginal ceremonial ground near Mabel Creek (50 km west of Coober Pedy).

1949

- In March of 1949, Len returned to Sydney and worked briefly as a surveyor with the Water Board. He received a letter from the LRWE on 17 November asking him to return to the Woomera Rocket Range project.

- Len's mother died of cancer in late August. Fortuitously, Len was at home during the last agonising months of her illness. Len was so grieved that he could hardly talk or carry on with his life.

1950

- In August, Len continued to survey the centreline of rocket fire to a distance of 160 kilometres north-west of Woomera and set out the Woomera Rocket Range.

- In the late summer of 1950, Len and a group of workers from the Line Construction Project Squadron at Woomera laid out a telephone line between the launching pad and Mt Eba. At the time, Mt Eba was the site of the furthest instrumentation tracking station. The men battled the relentless sun and intense heat for four months, completing the task on 4 April 1951.

1951

- In June, Len and a small party of scientists left Mabel Creek and headed north-west into the Great Victoria Desert. Their aim was to locate and mark the 250-mile point from the Woomera launching pad. An observation post, made of thick mulga and capped with a brass plate bearing the date, year and location (17 June 1951; latitude 28° 50' 20" S and longitude 133° 07' 23" E) was positioned at this point. Sheets of white canvas were also laid for a distance of nearly 8 metres from the post to form a cross which was visible from the air. It was intended that Mosquito bombers could fly along the centreline to follow and photograph the crosses. The aerial photographs were to be subsequently used to construct a strip map and plan tracking stations.

- Similar observation posts were later positioned at the 300-, 400- and 500-mile points along the centreline on 30 June, 16 July and 3 August respectively. (Their exact locations were: 300-mile point, latitude 28° 24' 28" and longitude 132° 27' 38", near Dingo Claypan; 400-mile point, latitude 27° 32' 09" and longitude 131° 09' 07", near Wright Hill; 500-mile point, latitude 26° 39' 07" and longitude 129° 51' 51", near Mt Harcus in the far north-west corner of South Australia). Another post was placed 550 miles from Woomera, but offset from the centreline (see Appendix). These observation posts became part of Len's 'bush signature'. A further series of signposts were erected at numerous locations throughout the Western Deserts of Australia during subsequent road-building activities (see Appendix).

• Len rediscovered Tallaringa Well on 5 June. The well had been an important watersource for Aboriginal people living on the eastern fringe of the Great Victoria Desert for centuries. The only white person to have visited the well previously was Richard Maurice on 15 May 1902. (Tallaringa Well is now the centrepiece of the Tallaringa Conservation Park).

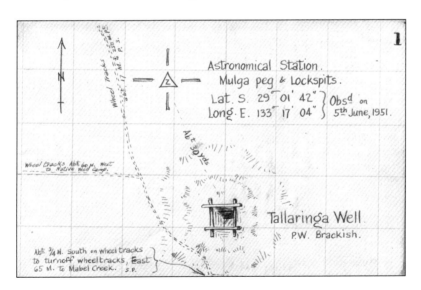

Len's pictorial description of Tallaringa Well, taken from his original field note book.

1952

• In mid-June, Len was summoned to the headquarters of the Long Range Weapons Establishment at Salisbury. He was told under a veil of secrecy that 'it had been decided to detonate an atomic bomb in Australia.' Len was given the task of selecting a suitable site for the blast. His only guidelines were that the site should not be closer than 30 kilometres at right angles to the centreline of the Woomera missile range and that there should be sufficient flat area around the site to establish a base and land an aircraft.

- In late August, around 285 kilometres west of Coober Pedy, Len found a large open area devoid of sandhills with a large claypan (approximately two kilometres long by one kilometre wide) nearby. The site was visited by Dr William Penney, Britain's chief nuclear scientist, together with a party of other government officials and scientists, in mid September. The site was given the tick of approval and soon became known as Emu, after a 'local inhabitant' who had implanted his footprint on the claypan. A village housing 400 army personnel sprang up at Emu over the ensuing months. The claypan was used as an airstrip throughout the subsequent nuclear programme.

Mark Shephard

Emu Claypan.

1953

- Ground access to the Emu area was urgently needed to bring heavy equipment to the site. Len spent the early part of 1953 (late February/early March) conducting reconnaissance work and bulldozing a track from Mabel Creek, past Tallaringa Well, to Emu. (This small section of road formed the beginning of the Anne Beadell Highway, which would later link Coober Pedy with the Western Australian goldfields).

- Two atomic bombs were detonated at Emu in October 1953. The first, codenamed Totem 1, was fired on 15 October and had an explosive yield of 10 kilotons. The second, Totem 2, was detonated on 27 October with a yield of 8 kilotons.

- The remoteness of Emu's location was creating a major logistical problem for the nuclear programme. A new site, which was less geographically isolated and had better access, was therefore sought. Following an 800-kilometre reconnaissance through the southern Great Victoria Desert during October, Len found a spot 35 kilometres north-north-west of Watson on the Transcontinental Railway line which he considered ideal for future atomic testing. The site became known as Maralinga, an Aboriginal word meaning thunder.

- From 29 October to 8 November, a track was bulldozed from the 300-mile point, along the centreline, to link with the track from Mabel Creek to Emu.

1954

- Most of Len's work during this year (and the first half of 1955) was spent preparing a contour map and developing the site of Maralinga. The new township comprised accommodation for 1 000 service personnel, a hospital, an airstrip, power generators and a distillation plant to convert salty bore water to fresh drinking water. Seven atomic bombs were detonated at

Maralinga over the subsequent three years *(see Table 1)*.

Table 1: Summary of British Nuclear-Weapons Testing in the Great Victoria Desert

Operation	Code name	Place	Date	Type	Yield (kilotons*)
Totem	Totem 1	Emu	15.10.53	Steel tower, 30 m	10
	Totem 2	Emu	27.10.53	Steel tower, 30 m	8
Buffalo	One Tree	Maralinga	27.9.56	Aluminium tower	15
	Marcoo	Maralinga	4.10.56	Ground surface	1.5
	Kite	Maralinga	11.10.56	Air burst (free-fall)	3
	Breakaway	Maralinga	22.10.56	Aluminium tower	10
Antler	Tadje	Maralinga	14.9.57	Aluminium tower	1
	Biak	Maralinga	25.9.57	Aluminium tower	6
	Taranaki	Maralinga	9.10.57	Air burst (balloon)	26.6

* one kiloton is equal to 1 000 tons of conventional explosive, TNT

1955

- During Len's stay at Maralinga, he assembled a party of six men to assist with future road-building projects. This party later became affectionately known as the Gunbarrel Road Construction Party (GRCP) and was subsequently responsible for the construction of over 6 000 kilometres of roads across Australia's Central and Western Deserts (see Chapter 7).

- From 11 August to 17 September 1955, Len conducted a reconnaissance and built a road linking Emu and Maralinga. He located and took an astrofix on Observatory Hill, a prominent 'bowl-shaped rocky knob' south of Emu, on 13 August. A signpost was erected on Observatory Hill on 3 September 1955; Len considered this to be the first of his 'real desert signposts.' He also found another Aboriginal ceremonial ground, which he later referred to in his books as 'Aboriginal Stonehenge.' (Note: this feature cannot be visited today unless prior written permission and a specific permit is obtained from

Len Beadell

The spectacular Rawlinson Range.

Maralinga Tjarutja, the traditional owners of this part of the Great Victoria Desert).

- A weather station was now needed to assist scientists at Maralinga to determine favourable atmospheric conditions for the detonation of bombs. From 13 November to 2 December, Len's party constructed a road from Victory Downs just over the Northern Territory-South Australia border to Mulga Park. This road formed the initial part of Len's most well-known landmark, the Gunbarrel Highway. The party continued westwards for a further 100 kilometres, reaching Mt Davies in the Tomkinson Range on 4 December.

- During an aerial reconnaissance of the country further west on 7 December, Len and Doug Stoneham selected the general area for the weather station in the south-eastern corner of the picturesque Rawlinson Range. Len, together with a party of four Land Rovers, set out from Mt Davies and reached the Rawlinson Range on 12 December, whereupon the exact location for the weather station was chosen. Len named the site Giles, after the well-known 19th century desert explorer Ernest Giles. (Giles Weather Station remains operational today and is the most remote meteorological station in Australia. The Gunbarrel Road Construction Party's grader is now permanently housed at Giles – see Chapter 14).

1956

- From February to March, Len's party pushed the Gunbarrel Highway westwards through the Musgrave, Mann and Tomkinson Ranges to Giles (which was reached on 29 March). The Gunbarrel Highway now stretched 600 kilometres from Victory Downs.

- The Giles village and airstrip were laid out during late April and May.

- Further roads were also required in the Great Victoria Desert as scientists wanted to capture radiation fallout north and west of Maralinga. On 26 June Len began a solo reconnaissance for another road from near Mt Davies in the north-western corner of South Australia, south-east across the northern Great Victoria Desert, towards Emu. Three days into the reconnaissance, he ran out of petrol six kilometres east of Wright Hill. He radioed

Mark Shephard

The awe-inspiring Mt Lindsay, the centrepiece of the picturesque Birksgate Range, along the Mt Davies Road.

to Maralinga for help and was retrieved on 4 July. Len continued his south-easterly sojourn with the retrieval team, but a broken rear axle and transmission failure to his vehicle the following day curtailed further reconnaissance work at a point around 110 kilometres north-west of Emu. After leaving his Land Rover in the desert, Len and the retrieval team finally reached Emu on 6 July. He left Maralinga on 14 July with parts to repair the Rover and was back at Emu again on 17 July.

* Len returned to Mt Davies on 23 July, ready to start construction work on the road south-east. A site for a mobile meteorological station was selected by Len on 10 August near Mt Lindsay, a prominent hill in the Birskgate Range. He took an astrofix for a further meteorological station near Coffin Hill on 26 August. Just over 275 kilometres of the road had been completed by 7 September, when work was temporarily ceased.

Jackie Junction on the Gunbarrel Highway. Len built a road linking Jackie Junction to the Aboriginal mission at Warburton in August 1958.

1957

- Len continued to work around the Giles Weather Station in the early part of 1957.

- Construction of the Mt Davies road recommenced on 27 June. The party arrived at a point 48 kilometres due west of Emu on 29 July. This location, known today as Anne's Corner (after Len's future wife), became the most southerly point of the Mt Davies Road. From here, the bulldozer was 'walked' eastward to Emu.

- In late October, Len undertook a reconnaissance to redirect part of the road from Emu across new country to Tallaringa Well and onto Mabel Creek; the new road was graded from 4 to 16 November. (The original road went directly past the Totem 1 and Totem 2 bomb sites, to the north-east of Emu Claypan. The new road was redirected five kilometres away from the bomb sites to arrive at the southern end of Emu Claypan).

1958

- From March to November, Len and his party completed reconnaissance and construction of the Gunbarrel Highway from Giles to Carnegie Station, through the very heart of the Gibson Desert. On 12 March, Len began a solo reconnaissance westward from Giles past Lake Christopher. The weather was oppressive over the next four days. According to Len's diary: 'It was red hot – 145 degrees in the cabin and the petrol was vaporising.' On 15 March, Len went to top up his vehicle's radiator with water and found, to his dismay, the container was empty. Using his bush survival skills to the fullest, Len was able to locate a small soak of water in an otherwise dry creek bed, which saved his life. He later found his way to Warburton Ranges Mission (hereafter referred to simply as Warburton).

- By 22 March, Len was back at Giles and leading the road

construction team westward. He arrived at a gravel tableland approximately 70 kilometres north of Warburton on 10 May; this location is known today as Jackie Junction (after Len's second daughter).

- Reconnaissance work on the final section of the Gunbarrel Highway, from Jackie Junction to Carnegie Station, was undertaken by Len and a team of other surveyors from 14-28 May. In late August, a road was built linking Jackie Junction to Warburton. Road construction of the last section of the Gunbarrel Highway commenced on 3 September. The party edged westwards past prominent landmarks such as Mt Charles (9 September), Mt Samuel (13 September), Mt Beadell (25 September; named after Len – see Chapter 14) and Everard Junction (around 15 October). Len and the GRCP finally pulled into Carnegie Station on 15 November. The 1 347 kilometre-long Gunbarrel Highway had taken three years and two days of interrupted work to complete. Central Australia and outback Western Australia were now officially linked by road for the first time.
(Note: today, prior written permission and a specific permit must be obtained from the Ngaanyatjarra Council, Alice Springs, to traverse the 280 kilometre section of the original Gunbarrel Highway from Giles to Jackie Junction via Lake Christopher. A more direct 230 kilometre section of new road now links Giles and Warburton. This road is known as the Warburton Road or the 'new' Gunbarrel Highway).

1959

- The early part of this year was taken up with continuing survey work around the Maralinga area.

- On 13 April, Len was presented with the British Empire Medal by Sir William Slim at Government House, Adelaide. The Medal was awarded in recognition of Len's outback surveying and road-building achievements thus far.

Peter Vernon

*Len at the magnificent
Bungabiddy Rockhole
on the Sandy Blight
Junction Road.*

*Len's signpost at
Mt Leisler, in the
early 1960s.
Note that
Tietkens' Tree
still has some foliage
at this time.*

Len Beadell

- From 1 June to 29 October, Len undertook a whirlwind around the world holiday (see Chapter 9).

1960

- From late March to early July, Len surveyed and constructed one of the most picturesque roads in the Australian outback – the Sandy Blight Junction Road. He named the road 'Sandy Blight' because he was constantly afflicted by an eye infection of the same name during reconnaissance work for the road.

    Construction of the Sandy Blight Junction Road commenced 30 kilometres east of Giles on 31 March. The party wound their way steadily northward, passing landmarks such as the breathtaking Schwerin Mural Crescent, Bungabiddy Rockhole in the Walter James Range (reached on 14 April), the Sir Frederick Range (19 May) and the Western Australian/Northern Territory border (10 June). Len also made an access road to the summit of the Sir Frederick Range. Construction continued north-easterly past the Davenport Hills (22 June) and the Tropic of Capricorn (25 June) before the team arrived at Mt Leisler on 29 June. A tree blazed by the explorer William Tietkens near the base of Mt Leisler in May 1889 was rediscovered by Len on his reconnaissance four days earlier. One of Len's trademark signposts was erected within metres of the blazed tree. The party passed the general area near Sandy Blight Junction on 4 July and continued the road for a further 26 kilometres, whereupon work was halted on 7 July. Len later selected the location for the present-day site of Sandy Blight Junction on 27 August 1960, following a three-day reconnaissance in the area. The last 26 kilometres of road were never used.

- On 27 August, Len began pushing a road due east from Sandy Blight Junction. It continued for 180 kilometres, and passed the Ehrenberg Range before joining station tracks near Mt Liebig, which was reached on 16 September. Len continued building the road due west from Sandy Blight Junction to the future site of Jupiter Well between 5 October and 7 November. (This section of road formed the initial part of what Len later called the Gary Junction Road, named after Len's only son Gary).

- On November 8, the GRCP's grader broke down near Jupiter Well. The grader, together with the party's 1 400 litre water tank and caravan, were hitched to the bulldozer, and an agonisingly long and slow haul back to Giles began. On November 12, the ration truck caught fire and was dragged off the road and left in the desert. For the next 14 days, the bulldozer towed its train at three kilometres an hour for 800 kilometres along the newly-built Gary Junction and Sandy Blight Junction Roads, before finally arriving at Giles on 26 November. Len described the event as 'the longest towing operation in the history of Central Australia.'

1961

- From 10 May to 6 June, Len built a small section of road linking the Gunbarrel Highway (near the Mann Ranges) to the Mt Davies Road (south-east of Mt Lindsay). The road became known as Kintore Avenue, as it passed close to a prominent hill, Mt Kintore.

- From 9 to 10 June, Len conducted a reconnaissance of the country west of Anne's Corner and pushed towards an isolated pinpoint on the map named Vokes Hill. The first white man to have visited Vokes Hill was the explorer Richard Maurice in July 1901.

- Len took a short leave of absence from his desert work to marry the new love of his life, Anne Matthews, on 1 July at All Souls Church, St Peters, Adelaide. Anne had first met Len during mid-1960, when her English parents rented Len's Salisbury home. Len was 38 and Anne was 20 (see End Notes).

Len with his young daughter Connie, who was wearing Dad's hat and boots.

Len, with his wife Anne and daughter Connie, pushed through the bush on a reconnaissance from Warburton to the future site of Neale Junction in July 1962.

Len Beadell

- Len was back in the Great Victoria Desert in late August, conducting a second reconnaissance in the Vokes Hill area. He found Vokes Hill on 28 August. Four days later, Len and his team began construction of the road from west of Anne's Corner to near Vokes Hill. His mission now was to complete a second road across Australia which would bisect the Great Victoria Desert approximately half-way between the Nullarbor Plain and the Gunbarrel Highway. Around 10 kilometres south-east of Vokes Hill, Len decided on a position for a major road intersection, which he named Vokes Hill Corner.

- On 23 September, Len commenced construction of a road due south from Vokes Hill Corner to Cook on the Transcontinental Railway line. The Vokes Hill Corner to Cook road was needed to provide further access to the railway line and to enable Native Patrol Officers to complete a rectangular loop through the Great Victoria Desert as part of their efforts to monitor movements of the desert's Aboriginal people. As part of his 'road-beautification scheme', Len guided the road passed a series of native Aboriginal wells, or watersources, including Waldana (27 September), Churina (29 September) and Bringyna (15 October). The road was completed on 20 November.

- Len's first child, a daughter Connie Sue, was born on 11 December 1961.

1962

- Len returned to Vokes Hill Corner in late March and began constructing the road further west on 2 April. Near the end of the month, Len and his party reached the eastern edge of the Serpentine Lakes. This chain of glistening white salt lakes, which wind for over 100 kilometres in a north-south direction along the South Australian-Western Australian border, presented a potentially formidable obstruction to the road's further progress. Len conducted a detailed reconnaissance of the area over the next few days, during which time he battled mountainous sandridges and furious heat. He found a narrow 100-metre strip of discoloured land between two large salt pans on 23 April. The following day he guided the bulldozer across the thin neck of land. The party reached the South Australian-Western Australian border within a kilometre of the western edge of the lake. A signpost was erected at the border on 25 April. The Anne Beadell Highway was now half completed. The team reached a point 93 kilometres west of the border on 7 May.

- Len left the party and returned to Adelaide for wife Anne's 21st birthday on 19 May.

- Accompanied by Anne and five-month-old daughter Connie (see End Notes), Len then travelled via the Stuart and Gunbarrel Highways to Warburton, arriving at the isolated mission on 2 July. The trio left the mission the next day and headed due south into the north-western Great Victoria Desert. Len's intention was to reach a point over 300 kilometres south, on the same latitude as the Anne Beadell Highway. From this point a 150-kilometre easterly course would lead them to the awaiting construction party. A week of solid travel brought the Beadell's to their southernmost point, which was soon to become a major road intersection known as Neale Junction. Len then headed his vehicle due east, while the construction team began to push west in response to regular radio messages and pistol flares. The two parties met on 11 July, 120 kilometres east of Neale Junction.

- On 14 July Len, Anne and Connie headed west on a 10-day reconnaissance to Yeo Lake, where they linked at a location known as Bonny's Hut with a sandalwood cutter's track which led south-west to Laverton. The Beadell's returned to the desert and rejoined the construction party east of Neale Junction. On 16 August, the head of the road reached Neale Junction, where a signpost is now erected.

- Work immediately commenced to survey and build a road due north from Neale Junction to Warburton. The 320-kilometre stretch of road, which passed numerous breakaways and flat-topped hills, was completed on 15 September. Len was back at Neale Junction on 27 September, preparing to head due south to the railway siding of Rawlinna on the edge of the Nullarbor Plain. After a month of hard work battling wind, dust, heat and flies, the party pulled in to Rawlinna on 23 October. A direct north-south road, which crossed 680 kilometres of the Great Victoria Desert and linked Warburton to Rawlinna, was now complete. The road was christened the Connie Sue Highway, after Len's daughter. Len drove Anne and Connie from Rawlinna back to Salisbury, and returned to the desert immediately.

- The final section of the Anne Beadell Highway between Neale Junction and Yeo Lake was then graded between 10 and 17 November. Construction of this major east-west road link, from Mabel Creek via Emu, Anne's Corner, Vokes Hill, the

Peter Vernon

The Gary Highway, built by Len in 1963, is one of Australia's great four-wheel-drive experiences.

Serpentine Lakes and Neale Junction to near Yeo Lake, had traversed over 1 065 kilometres of desert wilderness and spanned nine years and nine months of gruelling work.

1963

- The Beadell's first son, Gary, was born on 27 February.

- From 27 April to 18 May, Len surveyed and constructed a 340-kilometre section of road due north from Everard Junction (on the Gunbarrel Highway). The road was named the Gary Highway, after Len's newly-born son, and ended at a point called Gary Junction. His party then proceeded due east to link Gary Junction with Jupiter Well, which was reached on 25 May.

- From 4 to 21 July, Len's team built a road from Gary Junction heading north-west across the Canning Stock Route at Well 35, and through the heart of the Great Sandy Desert, to link up with the Callawa cattle station track.

- On 2 August, Len began a three-day reconnaissance east from the Old Talawana Homestead, past the Wells and McKay Ranges, to near Well 23 on the Canning Stock Route. On 4 August, near the McKay Range some 80 kilometres west of Well 23, Len encountered a group of around 40 Aboriginal people who had not seen a white man before. He showed elder members of the group his camera, radio, revolver and rifle, and drew a sketch of a dingo for them. Len described them as 'the happiest and most contented group of desert people I've ever had the pleasure to meet.' The following day he found Curara Soaks (Well 24). Len continued further east and, on 7 August, intersected the Gary Highway at a point around 190 kilometres north of Everard Junction. The wind howled incessantly for three days while Len waited for the construction team to catch up to him. 'Windy as fury', Len stated in his diary; it was little wonder he christened the location Windy Corner.

- After a six-week delay to fix a broken clutch on the grader, the party was back at Windy Corner on 24 September and ready to push the road west to Talawana. Well 23 was found by Len and Doug Stoneham on 29 September. Near the McKay Range, Len again stumbled upon the same group of Aboriginal people whom he'd met nearly a month before. An elderly Aboriginal gentleman, who had a profusion of body hair, also accompanied the group. Len befriended the man and affectionately named him 'Lolly.' Len was to meet up with Lolly two years later at Jiggalong Mission. The following day, October 3, the gearbox seized in the grader, necessitating almost a month's delay. Construction of the Windy Corner Road or Talawana Track [Len preferred to call it the former] recommenced on 30 October and was completed on 6 November.

The surveying and road-building feats of Len Beadell and his team, which had started somewhat innocuously over 10 years earlier, had finally come to an end – after spending far too long in the bush!

END NOTES

Letter of Employment with LWRE

Len received his official letter of appointment from the Long Range Weapons Establishment on 28 February 1950. It stated in part:

With reference to your application for a position on the staff of this Establishment, I have to inform you that approval has been given for your appointment to the position of Temporary Assistant Experimental Officer at this Establishment, with commencing actual salary of £483 per annum.

The salary of £483 at which you are offered appointment, comprises £359 per annum, including marginal allowance, plus £124 cost of living and basic wage adjustment.

Advancement within the range is subject to good conduct, diligence and efficiency in the performance of duties, and is by annual increments to the maximum of the salary range.

Cost of rail fares for yourself incurred in proceeding to South Australia will be borne by this Department. Accommodation could be arranged for you at the Long Range Weapons Establishment Hostel, Salisbury.

The Ultimate Irony

Few readers will know that the very man whose surveying skills were responsible for opening up much of the outback of Australia struggled with bureaucracy for nearly 10 years to gain registration as a surveyor.

The conflict arose because Len had failed to achieve the minimum educational standard necessary for registration; specifically, a pass in English at Leaving Certificate level was a compulsory component of registration.

John Richmond initially wrote to the Lands Department of Board of Surveyors of New South Wales on 21 January 1941. He requested that Len be granted special exemption to allow his registration as a surveyor, given the years of on-site training and experience Len had gained under Richmond's direction and his obvious penchant for surveying.

An extract from the Surveyor General of New South Wales' reply to Richmond on 4 February 1941 stated:

'[I] advise you that Regulation 7 of the Survey Examination Regulations, 1936, which sets out the preliminary educational standard necessary for entry into the profession, has always been very strictly interpreted by the Surveyors Board. It is unfortunate the Mr. Beadell, whom you find to be such a useful assistant, failed to obtain a pass at the necessary standard in the Leaving Certificate Examination, but this appears to be an insurmountable bar to his registration as a pupil. If you desire the matter placed before the Board, I could do so, but I cannot hold out any hope whatever for a favourable decision.'

Len's attempt to further pursue registration was put on hold due to the outbreak of the Second World War and his participation in the CSIR expedition to the Darwin-Katherine region in 1946.

In December 1947, Major (Bill) HA Johnson, one of Len's Commanding Officers in the army, and Dr Chris Christian, leader of the CSIR expedition, both wrote detailed letters to the Board of Surveyors of New South Wales recommending Len's surveying work and forwarding his case for registration.

Major Johnson wrote in part:

'Due to the nature of his work in the Survey Corps, Sgt. Beadell has had no opportunity of studying for matriculation during the period that he has served in the army – he has always been very ready to volunteer for any work which was difficult or demanding.

Sgt. Beadell is at present engaged on responsible work on the Woomera Range. Since it is an important point, I wish to add that men work well under him.

I should always be pleased to have him in any Unit of mine.'

Dr Christian added:

'Sgt. Beadell was attached to the CSIR Northern Australian Survey party during the survey of portion of the Northern Territory in 1946. His duties were the provision of ground control by astronomic observation, for mapping from aerial photographs. In this work he displayed a high degree of skill and extreme conscientiousness in securing exact data. He was obviously very much interested in all survey matters, and keen to make surveying his career.

Sgt. Beadell's character is beyond reproach; and I feel confident he would make a worthy member of the survey profession, which I understand is his desire.'

Mr H Coulson, Registrar of the Board of Surveyors, wrote to Len in April 1948 stating:

'Regarding your eligibility for registration as a pupil in surveying, I have to advise that your request has been considered by the Board of Surveyors, and I was directed to inform you that the Board is bound by the provisions of the Surveyors Act and Regulations thereunder, and could not register your articles unless you had previously attained the educational requirements prescribed in Regulation 4 of the Survey Examination Regulations, a copy of which is enclosed for your information.

I was also directed to advise you that the University has reduced its standard for Matriculation to certain ex-members of the Defence Forces, and has, to my knowledge, granted War Service Matriculation Certificates to a number of students who had passed the Leaving Certificate Examination or the Matriculation Examination in as few as three subjects. If these subjects included English, Mathematics I and Mathematics II the War Service Matriculation Certificate issued by the University would be acceptable to the Board for registration of articles as a pupil.

I would suggest that you might ascertain from the Sydney University their requirements for the granting of War Service Matriculation status to you. No such certificate would, however, be acceptable to the Surveyors Board unless it was based on a pass in English in addition to the two subjects already passed by you (which were Maths I and II, in 1941).'

Len then wrote to the University of Sydney in March 1949 and thereafter began a course in Leaving English and Geology. He was granted an extension of time until March 1950 to complete his War Service Matriculation Certificate. Len subsequently sat for the Leaving English examination on 15 November 1949 and Leaving Geology 10 days later.

By January 1950, the saga was concluded when Len received the following letter from the Registrar of the University of Sydney:

'I have to inform you that you have been granted war service matriculation status in order to proceed with Surveying.

This status has been granted you since you have obtained the following passes, Mathematics I and Mathematics II at the Leaving Certificate Examination of 1941, and English B, Geology B at the Leaving Certificate Examination of 1949, and have produced evidence of your war service.'

Anne Beadell relates the story of how she and Len met.

TOWARDS the end of 1959 Lenny decided that he would like to buy a house. He was spending most of the year in the bush camping, coming home to his base at WRE, Salisbury, for a couple of weeks in July, and taking his annual leave over Christmas. He would then head to the eastern states to visit his family and prepare his vehicle ready for the next foray into the desert in March. While in town he either stayed with friends (of which he had plenty) or simply slept in his car under a gum tree at WRE.

At the age of 38, he was getting a bit fed up with this and had a hankering to set up some sort of base where he could 'leave his axe.' He found a new house under construction that was to his liking at Salisbury, which was near his friends and work. Len's simple faith in humanity was illustrated by the fact that he paid cash for the house, got the builder to finish the garage so he could put his car in it, and then headed off to the bush for five months, trusting the builder to finish the house to his instructions.

My parents rented Len's house for a short time after migrating from England and that's how Lenny and I met. He knocked on the door one weekend in July and introduced himself. Everybody we met at Salisbury had told us about Lenny; he was the local character, a 'quiet clean-living man who must be quite religious because he didn't drink, smoke, gamble or go out with women.' We looked him up in *Who's Who*, so his achievements were known to us. But we were quite unprepared for the real Lenny we then met. We expected a rough sort of bloke, which he wasn't, or a 'toffy' British professional man, which he also wasn't! He came into his house and just gently took over our lives for a couple of weeks. He dug out his slide projector from the garage and showed us pictures of his work in the desert on the kitchen wall. We were enthralled and he talked for hours that first night. He then informed us that he would put his swag down in the empty spare room that had been locked for months.

I became fascinated by his life and asked if I could go on a trip with him. He said: 'Wee-yall, can you make an apple pie?' I assured him I could. When, in my naivety, I asked him what he did in the evenings in those long months away from civilisation, he replied: 'Oh, I do my tapestry!' Until I knew him better I really thought that was how he spent his spare time. I thought everybody finished work at 5pm and I didn't know his evenings were taken up with mending flat tyres, star observations and calculations until four in the morning. When I look back on those times I think of the countless hours I spent listening to him talk – and a lot of laughter.

I fell in love with his gentle manner which, to me at that time, was quite at odds with my idea of what a rough bushman should be. He was unfailingly good-humoured and, even at seven in the morning, was always ready for a laugh. He hated dissension or anything gloomy. Underneath it all, he lived for his work and I got caught up in his enthusiasm. We were engaged in February 1961 and married in July that year. He told me there might be 'a bit of fuss over this,' but I didn't foresee the havoc this announcement caused. I had apparently snared Adelaide's most

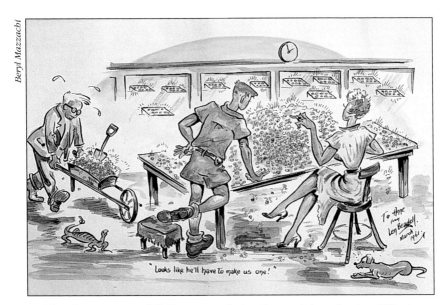

Beryl Mazzacchi

This classic Len Beadell illustration depicts Len and Anne having difficulty selecting an engagement ring!

eligible bachelor. Lenny was actually very shy with women and, apart from a crush on 'Dauby Dorothy' in primary school, he had never had a girlfriend. He was ready to share all his experiences with someone and I was the lucky one.

Anne Beadell describes her first bush experience with Len and daughter Connie in 1962.

FROM the first days of our marriage Len and I were determined to go to the bush together and I just couldn't wait to get out there. After Connie was born in December 1961, we accompanied Len for five months during the winter of 1962. This was our very first family desert trip. The two largest obstacles in getting to the bush were first gaining authority for Connie and I to travel in a Commonwealth vehicle, and secondly getting official approval for us to camp with Lenny's all-male Gunbarrel Road Construction Party. This proved to be quite a sticking point. In the end, Lenny convinced the authorities that most of his proposed work would be solo reconnaissance and therefore we would not be camping with the men. As he said: 'When we are out there we can do what we like'. And in reality, the boys were really quite pleased to have a baby along.

My mother also remained quite convinced that we were going to a waterless wasteland where her first grandchild would surely perish. My parents had no experience of Australia other than Adelaide and the northern suburbs. Unfortunately we left for the bush with her still convinced that this was the last she would see of us.

For the next five months, Connie and I led a blissful and surreal existence in the bush. Lenny resumed his reconnaissance of the east-west road which became the Anne Beadell Highway and we bush-bashed a southerly line from Warburton to Rawlinna on the Transcontinental Railway Line. This work resulted in the Connie Sue Highway.

Most days were spent in the vehicle, either driving cross-country, bashing through scrub or labouring over endless sandhills.

Len's daughters, Jacqui [far left] and Connie [far right], with Anne Beadell and well-known radio personality Ian McNamara, or 'Macca'.

Being winter, the days were mild but the cold nights were made comfortable by Lenny's generous campfires. As the weather grew warmer and the Construction Party caught up with us, Connie and I would sit on the soft red sand under the trees and absorb the solitude. Despite my mother's doubts, Connie thrived in this environment of total parental attention and clean fresh air. When we returned to Adelaide in October, she was ten months old and, as Lenny said, she had spent half her life in the bush! We were never in any doubt that we had done the right thing and this set the pattern for all our family bush trips some years later (see Chapter 11).

Chapter 6

$\mathscr{F}$AR TOO LONG IN THE BUSH

*T*HIS chapter presents an edited transcript of a lecture which Len gave to around 940 clubs/organisations around Australia over a 31-year period from 1964 to 1995. The lecture focuses on the establishment of the Woomera Rocket Range and the British Nuclear Testing programme. Len's character and unique sense of humour come to life as he describes, in his own words, the adventures of those years. To the countless thousands of Australians who were privileged to hear Len speak over the years, enjoy reliving the memory!

I WAS standing around a campfire 30 years ago on a freezing July night in the desert. I casually asked the fellow alongside me if there was anything wrong or whether something was troubling him.

He said: 'No, why should you think that?'

I replied: 'Oh well, it's just that you haven't said anything to anyone since February.'

He stated: 'Well I haven't got anything to say, have you?'

I said: 'Oh no, I don't suppose so.' And I left it at that until October and then I asked him: 'Are you sure there is nothing wrong?'

He said: 'You're always picking on me!'

That incident happened eight years after we drove up the old Stuart Highway to Alice Springs with our newly-formed group of workers that I called the Gunbarrel Road Construction Party. We were on our way to make a network of outback roads 4 000 miles long. (I'll talk in miles and gallons because I don't know what they are in kilopascals). Our aim was to open up over 1 000 000 square miles of central and Western Australia which had hardly been touched by white man, barring a few explorers. We came to an obstruction on the Stuart Highway; it was an enormous 40-ton truck bogged in the very middle of the road in a mulga scrub thicket. Our party just happened to have a bulldozer, a grader, and three 3-ton trucks with us. So we joined all these together, pulled the 40-ton truck out of the bog and parked it neatly alongside the road on a rocky outcrop. There was nobody about, of course, and so we bulldozed a lot of dirt in, graded it over, rolled it and carried on our way, leaving behind about 300 yards of the best piece of Stuart Highway all the way from Adelaide to Alice Springs. I often wondered what had happened to the driver of the truck. I found out several years later. After the truck became bogged, the driver thought: 'I'm not going to stay here.' So he walked to the next sheep station and hitched a ride on the Oodnadatta train to Adelaide. He told his boss he was quitting.

The boss said: 'Where's the truck?'

The driver replied: 'Oh, you'll find it bogged on the Stuart Highway.' I often wondered what the boss must have thought when he went up and found the truck neatly parked high and dry alongside the best piece of road on the whole highway.

But back to the real story. It all started in 1947 when I was casually asked if I would go and start a rocket range.

I said: Yes, I couldn't think of anything better. I'd always wanted to start a rocket range ever since I was four. By the way, what is a rocket range? I asked what they required and I was told 'a big area.' I said I knew where there was a million square miles of nothing. On enquiring when they wanted this rocket range built, they said: 'Straight away, right now!' I thought good, I won't even have to wait.

I was asked to go to Adelaide to meet a man by the name of General Sir John Evetts, who had been sent by Sir Winston Churchill to initiate the project. They told me what he looked like and I said, well, that's handy; I'll go and find him. The description they gave me left me in no doubt that I could find him. He was 8 feet high and 7 inches in diameter and I thought well, that pins it down. So I was walking along North Terrace in Adelaide and I saw him straight away. I went over to him, tapped him on the knee and said: Look, I've come to start a rocket range. He said:

'By jove, that's good.' That got rid of the formalities. He looked at a map of Australia. I told him I knew an area about a 100 miles the other side of Port Augusta that seemed fairly safe to launch a rocket. There was around a thousand and a half miles of country to the north-west across Australia where rockets could be fired with minimal risk.

So I drove up to Port Augusta with a jeep and a 3-ton truck. At that time I thought the project was going to last a fortnight; I didn't have any idea that it would occupy the entire rest of my working life for the next 40-odd years. I arrived at the general area where Woomera is now. I had the feeling that I wasn't hemmed in here. I discovered very quickly I could see a bull ant for 10 miles, unless he was lying down, and I thought now what a perfect area to start a rocket range. What a perfect area to start anything! The very first thing I did was to select a mountain near my camp which was nine inches higher than the rest of the plains. After climbing to its peak, I found that I could see a lot more of nothing from up there. I didn't even need oxygen. I put in a survey mark and spent a whole week high on the mountain, reading angles to give me a latitude and longitude from which I could start the whole project. Everything I did later in life – Maralinga, Emu and all the roads – was related to this one pin-point on the surface of the earth. Whenever one starts a rocket range of any sort, you must have a centreline along which the firing of rockets can take place. I chose a point in the middle of the Eighty Mile Beach between Broome and Port Hedland, a thousand and a half miles away to the north-west, and I worked out a bearing across Australia which would become the centreline of fire for the rockets. I didn't know at the time, but this centreline would govern the future of central and Western Australia forever; because I was to later open up a network of 4 000 miles of access roads to place instrumentation and carry out special surveys for satellite tracking stations, impact areas and target areas.

Every now and then I used to go into the local railway siding near Woomera and collect the latest urgent messages which would be telegraphed up to me. Yes, once a month I'd pick up these urgent messages. The first one said we must have a site for an airstrip. Visiting scientists have to come to this area. They've got to come quickly. Their time is valuable. I thought that's a bit elaborate for a one-night fireworks display. So I picked out a site for a runway which required the least amount of earthmoving, not a very hard task at Woomera. The next month's message said now we must have a site for a township. People have got to have somewhere to live while they're doing these experiments and we've got to have a town. I thought – a town! I was going to put up a tent fly to keep the sun off, but I thought, well, all right a township. I picked out a site which would be suitable for a village and did a survey there. This is where the Woomera township is today. The following month they said we're sending you up a 10 000 gallon water tank and I thought now that's a handy thing to have. I didn't know what I was going to put in it, but it would be handy for jumping into to keep out of the dust storms. It was slowly starting to sink in that this project was going to be a little bigger than I first imagined. After six months of living at Woomera and having the saltbush and gibber plains to myself, people started to come across the horizon with bulldozers and graders to build the airfield. I showed them the line of pegs that I'd put in across the saltbush and they started to construct the airfield. It was beginning to get too crowded for me. There were now 11 people at Woomera and I couldn't get to know everybody.

So I left them with their work and went on to examine the country over which the rockets would be passing, up to a distance of 550 miles from Woomera. I spent two years in the bush, on my own mostly, because I could never find anyone to come with me. I would stop every few days and eat a tin of bully beef using my cold chisel as a fork, in between taking star observations and mending six flat tyres a day.

The country west of the Stuart Highway is made up of solid mulga scrub and sandhills which roll on for hundreds of miles. The army eventually forced me to carry a transmitter. They said 'you're out there for months and months at a time. Nobody knows where you are. You could be pinned underneath a jeep and be seriously injured.' It would be a waste of a jeep.

Len in his trusted Land Rover on another solo reconnaissance in Australia's Western Desert country.

Two years after the transmitter was installed in the vehicle, I got my first message and I thought what a handy thing. I was ordered back to headquarters at Salisbury immediately. I thought, heavens, what have I done? I haven't upset anyone because I haven't seen anyone. I threw my swag into the jeep and I headed off through the sandhills. It took me a week to get back as far as the Stuart Highway. When I finally arrived in Adelaide, I was hustled into a little tiny office. Six people were standing there glaring at me. They drew the blinds and soldered the keyholes. The Chief Security Officer started the conversation in the most friendly way I'd heard for a long time, merely because I hadn't heard anyone for a long time! He said what we're going to tell you now is known to the six people in this room and nobody else. If it gets outside this room, it will be one of us and we'll find him and there will be a nine-year jail sentence. I thought, well, whatever you're going to tell me I might even keep it to myself. The Chief Scientist continued: 'We're going to explode an atomic bomb on mainland Australia and we want you to pick out a site.'

Is that all, I thought? And I expected it to be something important. They wanted the chosen site to be 'somewhere fairly well out of the way.' The centreline of my rocket range traversed some of the most remote country in Australia and so I thought, if I go 100 miles further out into the scrub, I'd be getting really well out of the way. That's where I headed and I spent five months searching an area of 30 000 square miles.

Purely by accident, I found Dingo Claypan, in amongst the monotonous sandhills. One glance told me that an aircraft of any weight could land on it. It was a perfectly natural runway in the wilderness, with no preparation required. I made this my base camp. But Dingo was only one mile from the centreline of rocket fire and five miles from the 300-mile point. So I searched out in all directions in a radius of about 100 miles from this claypan, trying to find an area free of sandhills and mulga scrub where we could detonate a bomb and erect a tent camp for people to live in.

Around 40 miles away I found an area where the sandhills diminished and the mulga scrub thinned out to open saltbush

A colour illustration drawn by Len, depicting his bush signpost overlooking Dingo Claypan.

paddocks. Within a few miles of this open area, there was a hard claypan around a mile in length, which could also support the weight of an aircraft. I thought this was a perfect site to explode a bomb and so I did a very careful astrofix and radioed the location down to the Chief Security Officer. It took me three days to work out that astrofix and five days to unscramble the code they had given me to enable transmission of the radio message.

I was then told a party of British scientists led by the most brilliant atomic scientist in the world at the time, Dr (later to become Sir) William Penney, were coming to inspect the bomb site I had selected. I thought now they'll be able to land on Dingo Claypan all right, but they won't know where it is; so I quickly radioed them the latitude and longitude of the claypan. They said they would be sending out two aeroplanes, one for the official party and the other full of spoons and forks. I thought I'd better order in another 12 cold chisels. At the same time, I thought I should requisition another eight brand new Land Rovers. The scientists could land on the claypan, but the bombsite was a further 40 miles away through the scrub; so they would need transport.

The Land Rovers were driven up to Coober Pedy. I made a new set of wheel tracks all the way back to the town, met the Land Rover drivers and guided them out to my claypan. My intention was to have all the Land Rovers on the spot and ready, like an instant Hertz Rent-a-Car service, when the scientists arrived. One of the drivers said to me: 'What are you going to do with all these Land Rovers. You've been out here for half a year. You suddenly say you'd rather like eight Land Rovers and they give them to you!' I couldn't tell him the real reason because I was thinking of the nine-year jail sentence. So I hurriedly said: 'Well, it will save me mending flat tyres; I won't have to mend a flat tyre for a long time.' Thereafter none of the drivers came near me. They were sure that I'd been too long in the bush.

I arranged for a Bristol Freighter to land on the claypan and take all the drivers away before the scientific team arrived. Due to the sensitive nature of the mission, the team chosen to pilot the freighter had to be hand-picked. They found an Air

Len leads a convoy of Land Rovers west from Mabel Creek.

Commodore whom I was assured had been a good pilot in 1918. He still had his wings but they were all moth-eaten. A visiting Air Vice-Marshall was selected as co-pilot. He'd also been behind a desk since 1918. And a poor little Group Captain was sent along to accompany them. To help them locate us in the bush, I made a huge mulgawood fire and threw a couple of staked rubber tyres on top. The burning rubber billowed off into the sky and formed a pencil of smoke which could be seen for a 100 miles in that country. On the morning of the freighter's impending arrival, the drivers and I stood looking in the direction of Woomera. Suddenly somebody saw the plane coming from the opposite direction. They'd missed us by 80 miles to the south and had decided to fly on to Fremantle, refuel and have another go. Luckily the Group Captain, acting as navigator, looked out of his side window. He saw a pencil of smoke on the horizon and tapped the Air Commodore on the shoulder. The aeroplane had to be turned around somehow. The pilot had a book put out by the Bristol people about how to fly the plane. The book said turn the wheel, pull back, push the pedal down and it should go around. So he thought: 'I'll try that.' And he did, and it worked. Finally the crew saw us on the claypan. The pilot circled around to come in for a landing. I didn't watch the touchdown because touchdown wasn't going to describe this landing. The plane bounced along the claypan one wheel at a time and stopped a mile away, just before it went into the sandhills. I later found out that Bristol Freighters can land and come to a stop in around 176 yards, but this pilot took the full mile. He taxied back across the claypan, jumped out and, with a beaming smile, asked me what I thought of the landing. I didn't know which one he was talking about. I said they were all right. His mouth took on a 20 past 8 shape. I said: 'don't look sad. Just think about what you've done. This claypan has never been seen by a white person since the world began and now, on this historic morning, you have made eight aeroplane landings on it.' We had to convince the Land Rover drivers to jump on to the plane for the return journey. We pushed them in and slammed the door quickly before they could escape. They took off and flew away in the general direction of Woomera.

I was left in the desert with eight brand new Land Rovers and no-one else for hundreds of miles in any direction. So I thought, I'll use this one on Monday and that one on Tuesday ... I never knew what to do with the eighth one.

On the night before the scientists were due to come, I looked down at myself for the first time in half a year and realised I looked scruffy. I had a shirt with no sleeves, but there was a button. I thought now that's handy because in April I remembered I saw a buttonhole; so if I put the two together I could keep off the westerlies. When I was talking to the scientists I would have to make sure I was always facing east. I couldn't do much about my pair of shorts because they were nearly torn to shreds. I had a pair of hobnail boots, which were tied up to two holes with kangaroo sinew. Every July and September I used to take them off in a hurry to empty out centipedes. It rained twice a year and, each time, the centipedes would find their way into my boots. I would tie them up to three holes for special occasions. When the Duke of Edinburgh came to Woomera, that was a three-hole job. I thought a pair of socks could make my whole appearance look a little neater. Of course I didn't have any, so I found an old pullover and some rags that I used to clean grease off the engine. I chopped the sleeves off with my axe. I thought these have got an added advantage to any other sock because I could put them on without even taking my boots off. So I pulled them up over my boots and bent the tops over with a pair of pliers: they were that stiff. Eventually I was all dressed for the official party, so I laid down in my swag on the claypan and waited.

I heard the drone of two aeroplanes at 4am the next morning. Unlike the previous flight, they came in for a perfect landing. The first person to get out of the aeroplane was one of the chief scientists, Alan Butement. You'd expect there to be a greeting – good morning, how are you, how's things or something like that. But all the chief scientist said was: 'Take those socks off, I can't concentrate.' So I pulled them over my boots and threw them on the ground. I was feeling more comfortable already. The first words that Sir William Penney said to me were: 'Would you do that again? I didn't catch that.' He said: 'I've never seen anybody take their socks off without first removing their boots.' I said they were special Australian socks and I showed him the loops and he was writing it all down. He said: 'They'll never believe me back in Aldermaston.'

The next morning when the sun came up, we set off in the Land Rovers for the bomb site. We drove 10 miles on the first day, that's how long it took me to walk back over every sandhill and bring their Land Rovers across one at a time. They'd never driven anywhere rougher than Piccadilly Circus. Eventually we arrived at the large claypan near the future bomb site.

That afternoon we walked around the edge of the claypan. One of the officers asked me what animal had made that footprint in the clay. I replied that it was an imprint of an emu's foot and, gradually over time, the site became known as the Emu Claypan. The following year when the first atomic bomb was exploded, the front page of every newspaper around the world stated the atomic test at Emu Claypan was successful.

One of the other scientists said: 'I've noticed something in common with these claypans. As the claypan dries out after rain,

Sir William Penney (left, with glasses) headed Britain's team of nuclear scientists at Emu and Maralinga.

A pictorial representation of Emu Claypan, taken from Len's original field note book.

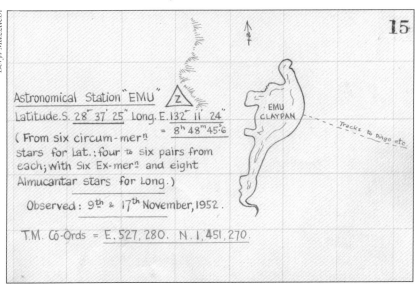

Beryl Mazzacchi

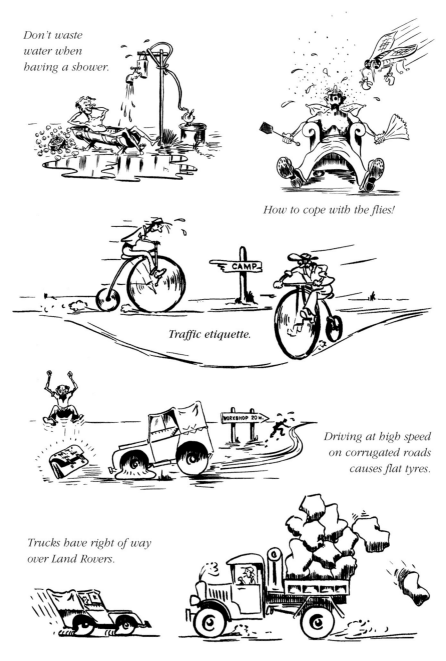

Don't waste water when having a shower.

How to cope with the flies!

Traffic etiquette.

Driving at high speed on corrugated roads causes flat tyres.

Trucks have right of way over Land Rovers.

Selected illustrations drawn by Len and taken from Welcome To The Claypan, *a booklet about camp procedures produced for all new service personnel on their arrival at Emu.*

the surface always cracks into pentagon shapes.' I said: 'Oh yes, they've got to crack in pentagons, they must do that.' They asked me why. I thought now when these sort of people ask you a question, you've got to answer them straight away. They used to say to me: 'Look here, when do these flies go away?' I would say: 'On the 18th April,' and they'd write that down. They were very precise sort of people and so, when they asked me why claypans crack in pentagons, I said: 'Well, it's all tied up with the lateral cohesion acting on the surface tension of the colloidal suspension of molecules of laterite.' They said: 'Oh, we see.' I thought thank heavens for that. Just then I was horrified. I looked down at my foot and there was an octagon right in front of me. I stood over it and my boots just covered it nicely. I didn't move for half an hour until they got back into their Land Rovers.

During the following year, 400 people descended on Emu Claypan. They brought everything needed to build the atomic site, including a hundred-foot steel tower with huge steel girders. The bomb was to be winched up to the top of the tower and exploded from there. I had to make a new road from the claypan back to the Stuart Highway because the atom bomb itself had to be brought up by road and all the required tracking instrumentation couldn't be carried on aeroplanes. A 52-ton centurion tank also came by road. The task of laying out the tracking instrumentation fell to me.

On the morning the bomb was to be exploded, I was instructed to go to the foot of the tower and join up two wires. I wasn't sure about this so I left my Land Rover a half an inch away from me and idling at five hundred thousand revs. I looked up and saw an ominous black atom bomb sitting on the top of the tower. There was a crow perched on top of it and I said to the crow: 'If I were you I'd shift.'

I went back to the central control area and stood alongside Sir William Penney when the bomb was exploded. The whole sky lit up with a blinding orange flash and I could feel the heat on the back of my neck. We turned around to see what had happened. There was a sheet of melted sand a half a mile long and the hundred-foot steel tower had turned into dust in less than a

Giles Weather Station, soon after its completion in 1956.

Len drew this illustration for the dinner menu at Emu.

A postcard from Giles, drawn by Len.

millionth of a second. I said: You can't leave anything lying around these days. You turn your back and it's gone!

I was then asked to select a new, more permanent atomic testing site at which a series of atom bombs could be exploded. The site had to be closer to the Nullarbor Plain to take advantage of rail access via the nearby Trans-Australian Railway line. I went on a 500-mile expedition to choose the new site which was called Maralinga.

I was then told we couldn't explode atomic bombs close to a major railway line without knowing where air movements are going to transport the radiation. 'Will you pick out a site for a weather station which will tell us this information?' they said. I asked where they wanted it and was told somewhere between Adelaide and Darwin. I looked at them and they looked at me quite anxiously. 'Do you think you could do it?' they said. I replied: 'Oh yes, I could jam it in there easily.' So I went 400 miles west of Alice Springs into the Rawlinson Range area and picked out a site for a weather station which we called Giles. The Giles Weather Station is still in operation today and it remains the most remote weather station in Australia. They then said: 'Will you make a road out to it; we can't find it.' So I assembled a small party of men, which later became known as the Gunbarrel Road Construction Party. We had a bulldozer driver, a grader driver, a cook and a long distance supply driver. We built the road from the Stuart Highway near the South Australian/Northern Territory border across the Musgrave, Mann, Tomkinson and Petermann Ranges to the Rawlinson Range; this was the very first road made into that country west of the Stuart Highway. To make the road, I went ahead on 500-mile return reconnaissance to find where I was going to locate it. I'd then come back and guide the bulldozer driver with a flashing mirror. The driver followed that flashing mirror for 8 years and never caught it. I was then asked to make 4 000 more miles of road. I said, 'yes, when would you like them?' They said: 'Straight away!' I thought, oh well, that's good. So I put my watch away and I stayed out there for another eight years building a network of 4 000 miles of roads, which were all focused on the original centreline of rocket fire from the

Woomera days. I continued the road I'd made to Giles another 500 miles west through the Gibson Desert. This road became known as the Gunbarrel Highway. Because I was opening up a million square miles of Australia for the first time, I thought I better keep it neat and so I built the roads in straight lines wherever I could, that is straight like the barrel of a gun. I then made another road from near Alice Springs to Marble Bar across the Great Sandy Desert and carried on the road I'd made to the Emu bomb site for another 800 miles across the Great Victoria Desert. I made a series of roads north from the Nullarbor Plain to intersect these east-west tracks. All in all, a million square miles of country. These roads are now widely used by Aboriginal communities, mining companies, mineral exploration and gas exploration workers, seismic survey teams and recreational four-wheel drivers; so it was quite a satisfying sort of a project.

All the work I did in Central Australia wasn't really a job to me. It was an absolute privilege to be allowed to do it. When you're given the whole of Central Australia to do with as you want for so long and to be able to shape its future, it's not work, it's a privilege and a pleasure.

END NOTES

A Potted History of Woomera

1946 The British and Australian governments joined forces to establish an experimental long range weapons testing range across Central Australia.

1947 Len Beadell chose the site for the rocket range and the flight path for rocket firings across Australia. The site for the range became known as Woomera, an Aboriginal word meaning spear-thrower. The whole area, officially known as the Woomera Prohibited Area, was later proclaimed. The 270 000 square kilometre area extended west and north west to reach across the Western Australian border and north to latitude 27°S.

The Long Range Weapons Establishment (LRWE) began operation at Salisbury, South Australia, with the aim of providing administrative and technical support to the rocket range at Woomera.

1948 Two thousand three hundred personnel were employed at Woomera to build a village, a rocket range and general range facilities. Woomera initially became a general-purpose weapons-testing range. Over the next few years several thousand British anti-aircraft missiles were fired from Woomera, aimed at un-manned radio-controlled targets.

1950 Woomera School first opened, with 33 pupils.

The first edition of the town's new local newspaper *Gibber Gabber* was printed on 11 August. Len contributed many articles and illustrations to the paper over the ensuing years.

1951 Range E was established as Woomera's main missile range. It became the best-equipped land range outside the territory of the superpowers. Nine independent and subsidiary ranges (A-G1) were developed at Woomera between 1948 and 1975 and, within these, over 15 numbered rocket and missile launching sites were established within the Woomera Prohibited Area. Range E remains in operation today for a variety of defence and commercial activities.

1955 An internal structural reorganisation within the Department of Supply saw the Weapons Research Establishment supersede the Long Range Weapons Establishment at Salisbury.

1958 The Black Knight rocket, standing over 10 metres tall and one metre wide and costing £5 million, was fired from Woomera on 7 September. At the time, it was the largest rocket to have been launched from Woomera.

1960 The development of an intercontinental ballistic missile (ICBM), known as Blue Streak, had become a major project of the British Government in the late 1950s. However, the project was abandoned by the British on 13 April 1960 before a single test flight had taken place at Woomera. The Blue Streak missile itself was 21 metres long and three metres wide.

1964 The first trial of the European Launcher Development Organisation (ELDO) project took place on 30 April. The ELDO project ultimately failed in its numerous attempts to launch a satellite into space over the next six years. The Blue Streak was used as the first stage for all ten of the Europa 1 rocket launches. The Europa, standing over 30 metres tall, three metres wide and weighing 106 tonnes, became the largest rocket to be launched from Woomera.

Woomera was in its heyday during the mid to late 1960s, with a population of around 6 000.

1967 The 21-metre American Redstone rocket, carrying the Australian-designed and built WRESAT satellite, was launched from Woomera on 29 November 1967. WRESAT became the first and only satellite launched by Australia. The 70kg satellite, displaying a white kangaroo emblem, finally burnt out over the Atlantic Ocean on 10 January 1968. The first stage of the Redstone rocket crashed into the Simpson Desert and was recovered by a team of volunteers in April 1990. It remains on display at the Woomera outdoor missile park, opposite the town's Heritage Centre.

1969 An agreement between the United States and Australian governments to establish a satellite ground station at Nurrungar, 19km from Woomera, was signed on 10 November 1969. Nurrungar is now one of the three most important joint United States – Australia defence, scientific and intelligence facilities in Australia (along with Pine Gap and North West Cape). Today more than 500 Australians and Americans are employed at Nurrungar and live in the Woomera village.

1971 The British satellite Prosperoe was launched from Woomera in October, as part of the Black Arrow Project. The Prosperoe satellite is still in orbit today.

1972 Around 40% of the original Woomera Prohibited Area, including the opal-mining townships of Coober Pedy and Andamooka, was de-restricted. The Woomera Prohibited Area now covers 127 000 square kilometres and represents possibly the largest land-locked rocket range in the world. Persons wishing to travel across the Woomera Prohibited Area must first obtain a permit from the Range Liaison Officer, Box 157 DSCW, Woomera, SA 5720.

1982 The Woomera Primary and High Schools amalgamated to become the Woomera Area School.
The township of Woomera became de-restricted and open to the general public.

1987 A series of seven sounding rockets (six NASA and one West German) were launched from Woomera to study UV rays emitted from Supernova 1987a, a star that exploded 170 000 years ago but only became visible to world scientists in February 1987.

1992 The population of Woomera was estimated at around 1 500.

1995 NASA returned to Woomera to launch another series of sounding rockets.

1996 The Japanese space agency NASOA carried out thirteen successful flights of their model space plane called ALFLEX (Automatic Landing Flight Experiment).

1997 The town of Woomera celebrated its 50th birthday on 1 April. Woomera hosted Exercise Ready Shield 97, the largest Australian Defence Force military exercise since the Second World War. Exercise Ready Shield involved the mobilisation of over 3 000 troops belonging to the 6th Brigade.

Source of material: The History of Woomera *(available from the Woomera Heritage Centre) and* Woomera – Our Outback Space Town *(article written by Paul Raffaele and published in Australian Geographic 12, Oct-Dec 1988, p 98-115).*

Chapter 7

$\mathcal{T}$HE GUNBARREL ROAD CONSTRUCTION PARTY

D OUG Stoneham is one of the few surviving members of the original Gunbarrel Road Construction Party (GRCP). Doug was employed by the Department of Works and drove the D-8 bulldozer during construction of the Emu to Maralinga Road, the Gunbarrel Highway, the Sandy Blight Junction Road and the Mt Davies Road. He left the GRCP in August 1960 when he married his wife, Margaret, but later rejoined the team in late 1963 to complete the Windy Corner Road. Doug retired from the Department of Works in 1991, after 43 years service. He and Len remained good friends for over 35 years.

Doug reflects on the road construction days and provides an insider's view into the characters who made up the team, including Len.

Doug Stoneham (right), with Len's daughter Connie at one of Len's bush signposts near the Schwerin Mural Crescent.

It was back in 1955 that I was first approached to go to Maralinga. I had been employed by the Department of Works since 1948, where I had worked as a bulldozer driver on projects at the Adelaide Airport, Leigh Creek, Whyalla, Mt Gambier and Renmark. While at Renmark, one of the Department's engineers, Paris Drake-Brockman, was seconded to the Maralinga project. He asked myself, Scotty Boord (a grader driver with whom I had worked previously) and five other members of the Department to accompany him.

We soon boarded the 'tea and sugar' train at Woomera, destined for Watson. It was during this train ride that I first encountered my future boss, Len Beadell. I wondered who on earth I'd come across. He looked like a hillbilly with his shorts, belt and no hat. He bounded around the train, patting dogs on the head, carrying children and pinching the sugar.

Scotty Boord and I were initially assigned to work with Len on building a road linking Maralinga and Emu. After completing the task, Len came up to us one day and asked whether we'd like to continue to work with him on building thousands of kilometres of other new roads in the outback. We were both single at the time and had no commitments; so we readily accepted his offer.

Len assembled a team which initially comprised myself (as bulldozer driver), Scotty (grader driver), Bill Lloyd (supply driver), Rex Flatman (general mechanic), Willy Appleton (cherry-picker), and Paul Christensen (cook). Several members of the team were replaced as the years went on. Frank Quinn became our supply driver. Other cooks including Cyril Koch and Tom Roberts accompanied the team for short periods. 'Shorty' Williams took over from Scotty towards the end of the road-building era, and Eric Graefling succeeded Billy Appleton. Len, of course, remained leader of the GRCP throughout.

We all enjoyed Len's company as our boss. He was forever bright and cheerful. He looked after his men well and always ensured we had the supplies and equipment we needed. He treated everyone fairly and acted as peacemaker in any disputes which arose from time to time. He even pulled our teeth and cut our hair! (see End Notes).

As everyone knows, Len was a great storyteller around the campfire. He didn't mind us telling jokes too, as long as they weren't smutty (which was pretty hard when there were only ever blokes around the campfire). But Len had strong principles and he stuck to them, even out in the middle of the desert. He didn't smoke and never drank. In fact, he always used to lock the waterbag which hung on the front of his vehicle, in case one of the boys tried to doctor its contents.

But seriously, though, Len was a really good boss and leader of men. He also had a good crew of men around him, and our road building achievements were a real team effort. Everyone contributed to the success of our work and, for the most part, we all got on well; we had to, there was no-one else to talk to!

Scotty Boord stayed with Len throughout the subsequent road building years until he eventually got a hernia through constantly lifting heavy grader tyres. He was very quiet and sombre by nature, but always got the job done.

Rex Flatman was a fitter and heavy equipment mechanic of the highest calibre. He was responsible for servicing the bulldozer, the grader, our refrigeration equipment, the cherry picker's Land Rover, and our three Commer trucks. (One of the trucks carried food, one was used as a service wagon by Rex, and the other was our supply vehicle). Rex never did anything by half measures; he was always thorough and meticulous.

Frank Quinn was an outstanding supply driver. His job was to bring fuel, rations and water to our flying camps every month.

Len at the helm of the Gunbarrel Road Construction Party.

Len Beadell

Scotty Boord, bulldozing a new road near the camp at Emu.

Mind you, he'd had plenty of experience before joining our team. He'd been the mail driver around the Northern Territory/South Australian border for many years and, prior to that, he'd carted cattle, wool, drums of fuel and sheep dip around the outback for most of his life.

I'll never forget the first time I saw his vehicle. He brought a load of fuel to our camp at Mt Davies after travelling 600 miles from Kulgera, the last 300 of which was ungraded. The truck had no cabin; Quinny just sat on a box in the open! It was the 'biggest heap of rubbish' I'd ever seen. The transmission had fallen out along the way. Quinny simply removed the front bumper bar and bolted it across the chassis to hold the transmission in place.

Nothing ever fazed or worried Quinny. He was a real happy-go-lucky character who got on well with everyone, especially Len. And nothing could stop him from getting the job done. On another occasion, a mulga stick penetrated the radiator of his old truck. He removed the radiator, got a hose, connected one end of the hose to the engine block and the other to a 250-litre water tank which sat behind his seat, and continued on his way. The

The enterprising 'Quinny', a real bush mechanic.

Doug Stoneham, covered in grease and hard at work in the bush.

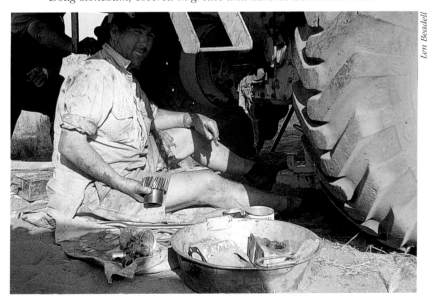

water in the tank was boiling by the time he had travelled a couple of hundred miles to reach our camp, but he got there!

Willy Appleton was the party's 'cherry-picker' driver; his job was to hand-pick any sticks, roots or stones left after the final grading of a new section of road. Bill was a good bloke, but he could be a bit scatter-brained at times. One night during the building of the Mt Davies Road, we were setting up our mess tent after a hard day's work. The ground was so hard that we could only get three of the four tent pegs into the ground. Willy tied the remaining peg to the draw bar at the rear of his Land Rover. After our meal was completed, Willy walked out of the tent, stepped over the tent rope leading from the draw bar, and hopped into the vehicle. He then headed off down the track. The Land Rover seemed to be making hard work of it, so Willy put it into four-wheel-drive. He looked in his rear vision mirror to see the tent dragging behind the vehicle and the remainder of the party shaking their fists in anger!

Another time, we had left some oil five miles back on the road, along with two cases of grapefruit juice which we had been carrying for the past two years. Len sent Willy back to retrieve the oil. En route, his radiator boiled. The enterprising Willy decided to pour the grapefruit juice into the radiator, tin by tin every quarter of a mile. When he arrived back in camp, the engine was encased in a hot sugary clag and smelt like a candy factory.

Paul Christensen, our cook, contracted polio when he was a child and therefore, although he was a big man, he struggled with his legs. He had worked previously as a shearer's cook and first met Len at Woomera. I really enjoyed Paul's cooking over all those years and he especially made a good damper, or 'survey cake' as Len called it. If you didn't like what Paul served up, then he would simply say: 'Go and get yourself a tin of bully beef.'

In summing up my years with the GRCP, I would certainly have to say that we worked hard and put in very long hours. The intense heat for three quarters of the year, the clouds of flies and the never-ending isolation also made our working conditions difficult. But I loved every minute of it. I'd get up in the morning and there was my dozer next to me. I didn't have to travel to work and push through heavy traffic. I worked hard all day and then enjoyed free tucker, a shower, and a tin of juice at night. As Len always told us, we were making the maps obsolete on a daily basis and creating our own piece of history. And when we finished, everyone would follow in the tracks which we had made.

It was perhaps fitting that Doug was there at the very end of the Gunbarrel Road Construction Party's work in November 1963. Doug was called back to help the party and drive the grader during the last stages of the construction of the Windy Corner Road. He then drove the grader back to its final resting place at Giles Weather Station.

END NOTES

What's in a Name?

Len described the origin of the name 'Gunbarrel Road Construction Party' in an article published in the October-December 1960 issue of Missile.

H E stated: After we had started Woomera and later Maralinga, we gradually got together what I later called *The Gunbarrel Road Construction Party,* a rugged-sounding name stemming back to incidents which happened to me in 1947. All the country around the Woomera area was then getting over the effects of an unusual flood in 1946. It was still very boggy, everywhere except on gibbers between the salt-bush. I would, as a result, endeavour to keep to the stones only, while driving constantly over it in my Jeep. As people came and a town appeared on the prairies, they all followed my exceptionally twisting wheel tracks instead of going anywhere as was possible when things dried out. You can see a bull ant for ten miles in that country, but still the same tracks were used. I heard so many remarks about people being able to see their own tail lights, snakes unable to negotiate the turns,

Len drew this illustration for the Morton family of Victory Downs, during the initial stages of construction of the Gunbarrel Highway.

good job differentials were invented and so on. I repeated the reason so many times, that I have been going dead straight every since. Later when we came to actually build all these roads in the Centre, I made them perfectly straight wherever possible, some thirty miles at a time without a curve. Straight as a gunbarrel.

Len the Barber

LEN had three categories of haircut, 'Adelaide in five days' (a fairly close crew-cut), 'Adelaide in one month' (a stubble crew-cut), and 'Adelaide in four months' (shaved bald). After seeing the four-month style, one of Len's cherry pickers remarked that a six-month one would make the customer resemble an aristocrat caught in the French Revolution! Len also used to joke about the time an English serviceman approached him for a haircut at Emu, prior to his returning home to the Mother Country. Len asked whether he wanted a 'London in four months'. One micro-second later, Len was on his own with clippers poised, looking at a vacant oil tin barber's chair.

Len the Bush Dentist

MANY readers will know that Len fancied himself highly as a bush dentist. With the Gunbarrel Road Construction Party being away from civilisation and in the bush for months at a time, Len felt that dentistry would be a handy skill to master. He had often seen how toothache could affect men living in the bush.

In June 1957 Adelaide-based dental surgeon Bruce Dunstan flew to Woomera to perform fillings on local personnel, including Len. Bruce gave Len a crash course in dentistry during this visit. He also received dentistry tips from Alice Springs dentist, Ray Meldrum. Len soon acquired all the equipment and anaesthetics needed for his bush dentistry kit.

"OH! JUST A FEW THINGS RAY GAVE ME .... IN CASE I HAVE TO MEND A DENTURE."

Len drew the above illustration for Ray Meldrum. Ray provides some background on the illustration: 'Len initially approached me for some dental supplies and local anaesthetics. I gave him some practice at extracting teeth on several occasions and found him to be very competent. It would have been a worry if he had decided to set up in opposition in town! I also showed him how to repair dentures and gave him a kit of repair materials and instruments which he fitted into a small box (30cmx30cmx20cm) in his Land Rover. On his next trip to the Alice he presented me with this cartoon, showing the denture repair kit enlarged to fill a trailer. The cartoon was painted with a child's set of water colours and some precious water in a billy can, while Len was sitting beside his Land Rover some 700 km from the nearest civilisation.'

Getting down to the specifics, Len performed his first tooth extraction on 25 March 1958, when he removed the right eye tooth of Cyril Koch. At the time, Cyril was accompanying Len's party as they headed east from Giles and past the Rawlinson Ranges during construction of the Gunbarrel Highway. Len extracted a further six teeth from Cyril on 2 April 1958! Scotty Boord was Len's next patient, two days later on 4 April. Len pulled a total of 29 teeth from various sufferers over the ensuing years. He proudly told stories of how he had '29 notches on his forceps' and he made meticulous diary entries recording exactly which teeth had been removed.

Chapter 8

$\mathcal{D}$ESERT LIFE TAKES ITS TOLL

T HE year 1964 provided quite a change of pace for Len. On 9 January he gave the first of around 940 lectures on his Outback exploits to the Salisbury Rotary Club at Elizabeth. He spent much of the year commuting by aeroplane between Adelaide and Woomera. His work at Woomera centred around carrying out astronomical observations and positioning tracking instruments for the ELDO rocket programme. He worked alone at a site around 15 kilometres from the town. Anne, Connie and Gary regularly drove up to Woomera to be with Len for several days at a time. At night while staying at Woomera, Len worked on the manuscript for his first book *Too Long in the Bush*, which he had started writing in September 1963 during construction of the Windy Corner Road. The book described the building of the Gunbarrel Highway and the establishment of Giles Weather Station. He would write for one week and then spend the following week typing up what he had written. He brought a small portable typewriter with him on his 'typing week' and would sit up until the early hours of the morning, tapping out pages of text one finger at a time. The writing of *Too Long in the Bush* was completed on 8 October 1964 and the book was released in November the following year. Towards the end of 1964, the weather at Woomera became oppressively hot. Len noticed that he began to struggle to keep up with his daily work at the rocket site. By the end of each afternoon he had difficulty simply dragging one hob-nailed boot in front of the other. His face became yellow and bloated and he had fever, diarrhoea and a sore chest. It was the first indication that Len had contracted hepatitis, a debilitating illness which was to cause him even greater hardship the following year.

Early in 1965 Professor Donald Thomson, who was Chair of

Len Beadell

Donald Thomson's daughter, Louise, at Jupiter Well.

Thomson and his daughter at Well 35 on the Canning Stock Route.

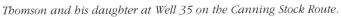

Len Beadell

Anthropology at Melbourne University, visited the Salisbury headquarters of the Weapons Research Establishment. Professor Thomson had learned of Len's 1963 encounter with a group of Gibson Desert Aboriginal people near the McKay Range. He wanted Len to accompany him on an expedition to relocate the group and was determined to study them. He even brought a letter signed by the then Prime Minister, Sir Robert Menzies, requesting that Len be seconded for this task. Len described Professor Thomson as 'a tiger of a bloke, a little livewire.'

As always, Len was keen to revisit the bush and promptly requisitioned his trusted Land Rover from the workshop. The vehicle had taken a real hammering from the last period of Len's roadmaking activities and had required a major mechanical overhaul. Professor Thomson had brought two as-new International four-wheel drive vehicles with him in readiness for the trip.

Len and Thomson, accompanied by Thomson's young daughter Louise, left Adelaide on 25 February for a three-week, 10 000 kilometre whirlwind trek via the Gibson and Great Sandy Deserts to the Windy Corner Road and back. When Len finished his roadbuilding feats in 1963 he was unsure when he would have the opportunity to revisit the desert country he loved so passionately. He was therefore very excited to be once again traversing his own roads just over a year after they were completed. The roads were generally in excellent condition, with no evidence of washaways or damage.

The party arrived at Ethel Creek Station on 9 March, after travelling via Coober Pedy, Musgrave Park, Giles, Mt Leisler, Jupiter Well, Well 35 on the Canning Stock Route and Marble Bar. George Anderson, the owner of Ethel Creek Station, was keen to accompany the party along the Windy Corner Road in search of the Aboriginal people. He had lived in the area all his life, but had never been east into the heart of the desert. Several Aboriginal station workers also came in Anderson's vehicle.

As the combined party drew near the McKay Range, several spinifex fires were seen. A search of the nearby area found evidence of fresh diggings in a small soak. Two Aboriginal elders

The party's vehicle bogged near the McKay Range on the Windy Corner Road,
10 March 1965.

suddenly emerged from the nearby scrub, followed by around
eight further Aboriginal people. They remembered Len from their
initial encounter two years ago, while Len himself was excited by
the reunion. The elders led Len's group to a rockpool where
several galahs were drinking. Everyone sat down in the sand.
The Aboriginal people from Ethel Creek Station initially sat with
their backs to the desert inhabitants but, within about 15 minutes,
the two groups began to communicate with each other and were
soon laughing and exchanging stories. In 1963 when Len first
made contact with the nomadic group, their numbers comprised
around 40; however now only around ten people remained living
a traditional lifestyle. Len later learnt that a number of the group
had recently come out of the desert and were residing at Jiggalong
Mission, around 80 kilometres south-east of Ethel Creek. Len felt
a touch of sadness at that point, because he realised the traditional
life style which these people had been living for centuries had
now been broken by white contact. Professor Thomson was
nonetheless overjoyed by the rendezvous and spent considerable

time talking to, and recording information on, the group.

After saying goodbye to the desert Aboriginals, Len and Professor Thomson headed for Jiggalong Mission. Len's physical condition again worsened. His face was yellow and swollen, his throat and neck was inflamed, his eyelids were coated with a sticky fluid and his legs were swollen with cellulitis. He barely had enough energy to drag his body across to the campfire at night. The nursing sister at Jiggalong insisted that Len leave his vehicle at the mission and be flown back to Adelaide by the Flying Doctor Service. Len refused saying: 'I've only got another 2 000 miles to go to get home.' Against medical advice, the pair headed along the Gary Highway to Warburton. Another nurse at Warburton pleaded similarly with Len 'not to go an inch further.' But Len replied: 'I've got a thousand miles less to go, now!' After travelling via Giles, Musgrave Park and Woomera, Len finally arrived back in Adelaide on 18 March in considerably worse health. He was diagnosed by a local doctor (Dr Hart) as having beriberi, a form of malnutrition resultant from a dietary lack of vitamin B1 (thiamin). Len was then referred to a leading specialist, Dr Robert Hecker, who immediately placed him in the Memorial Hospital. He stayed there from 10 April to 1 May. A number of tests were carried out, including a liver biopsy, barium meal and numerous X-rays. Len was diagnosed as having chronic active hepatitis B, partly attributable to sustained malnutrition. His countless years in the bush living on a diet of tinned bully beef had finally taken their toll.

Len managed to retain his spirit and sense of humour throughout the period of hospitalisation, and never wasted a spare moment. He drew a watercolour painting for Dr Hecker. It portrayed a nurse, armed with a sledge hammer and crowbar, taking a biopsy sample from Len. As blood trickled down Len's side and into a bucket, it was simultaneously being drunk by Len's goanna friend! The picture held pride of place on the wall of Dr Hecker's office for many years. Len also worked on final drawings for *Too Long in the Bush* and liaised with his publisher, Rigby, during his hospital stay. Len proved to be a notoriously mischievous patient and he played havoc with the nursing staff.

Len was ordered not to have any salt in his diet. However he would regularly borrow some from other patients, hide it in his bedside drawer and sprinkle it on his eggs for breakfast. He also disliked the nurses 'fluttering about' and constantly interrupting him. In quiet moments, he often looked out of the hospital window across the adjacent parklands and yearned to be back in the bush.

Amid this upheaval, Len's wife Anne was imminently expecting the birth of their third child. Len was discharged from the Memorial Hospital on 1 May, with instructions to not resume work for three months. Dr Hecker later told Len the results of his liver biopsy were so bad that he didn't think Len would have ever been able to leave hospital. Six days later, at 5.10am on 7 May 1965, the Beadell's second daughter, Jacqueline, was born at the Lyell McEwin Hospital, Elizabeth.

Len was required to see Dr Hecker on a regular basis for three years thereafter. It took this length of time for Len's liver function to return to normal. During this period, Len was rushed to Memorial Hospital on four separate occasions suffering from severe infections and raging temperatures. Each time his bare skin was wrapped with pillowcases full of crushed ice to bring down his body temperature.

On 12 July 1965, Len resumed light duties at the Weapons Research Establishment. He had been seconded to the Facilities Drawing Office since June the previous year, but did not enjoy his time there. It was not until 22 May 1967 that Len moved to the Illustration Section at WRE on a permanent basis. Len really enjoyed working in this area and spent the remainder of his career attached to that section. The work was always interesting and challenging. He was involved in preparing graphic material for major exhibitions and for scientific staff presenting lectures at conferences.

END NOTES

Professor Donald Thomson

Donald Finlay Ferguson Thomson (1901-1970) is widely regarded as one of Australia's pre-eminent anthropologists. Between 1928 and 1933, he undertook three major scientific/anthropological expeditions to Cape York, in Far North Queensland. In 1957 and 1963 he also conducted detailed anthropological studies of the Pintupi people of the Western Desert region of Australia. This work resulted in the publication of several hallmark scientific papers most notably *The Bindibu Expedition - exploration among the Desert Aborigines of Western Australia*. Geographical Journal 78, parts 1, 2 and 3, 1972, as well as a book entitled *Bindibu Country* (Nelson, Melbourne, 1975). Donald Thomson was appointed Professor of Anthropology at the University of Melbourne in 1962. He was also awarded a Doctor of Science, and gold medals from the Royal Anthropological Institute, the Royal Geographical Society and the Australian Geographical Society.

Source: *Encyclopedia of Aboriginal Australia (Nelson, Australia, 1995).*

Examples of classic Len Beadell illustrations taken from Too Long In The Bush *(top) and* Blast The Bush *(bottom).*

Len at work at night, ably assisted by his lizard friend.

Len sweating it out when first told about the nuclear testing programme.

Chapter 9

$\mathcal{A}$ WRITING FRENZY

THE year 1966 marked the beginning of a decade and a half during which Len wrote five further books detailing his road-building exploits and hilarious outback adventures. Altogether, the books comprised more than half a million words. Len began this writing frenzy in response to an expression of interest from Rigby's Editor-in-Chief, Ian Mudie, after Ian had seen Len interviewed by Robert Caldicott on ABC television.

Blast the Bush was penned after *Too Long in the Bush*. The book described the setting up of Emu and Maralinga for the British Nuclear Testing Programme and gave a vivid account of the first atomic explosion at Emu.

Len commenced writing *Blast the Bush* on 4 January 1966, during one of his enforced stays in Memorial Hospital following a fever attack. He recalled: 'Anne brought my typewriter in and I used to tap away freely until the nurses said the noise was disturbing other patients. So I sat quietly in my chair and wrote a whole chapter for the book during one night from 9pm to 6am. I was on a roll that night and couldn't put my pen down.' The writing of *Blast the Bush* was duly completed in hospital on 17 March 1966. It was released on 6 May 1967 and proved an instant best-seller, much to the delight of Len's publisher, Rigby.

Len was ready to hang up his pen, but Ian Mudie, and Rigby's Managing Director, Merv Branson, were persuasive in twisting Len's arm to continue writing. They felt Len had 'at least another ten books in him.'

Every spare moment in Len's life was now occupied with writing. He found a hard-working ally in Glenys Szarmanski, from the WRE, who spent countless hours typing up Len's hand-written draft manuscripts. The writing of *Bush Bashers* was commenced on 26 March 1968 and completed on 18 September the following year. It was first available in book shops on 23 April 1971. *Bush Bashers* documented the story of the building of the Anne Beadell and Connie Sue Highways. *Still in the Bush, Beating About The Bush,* and *Outback Highways* followed during the 1970s. *Still in the Bush* was penned between 26 January 1972 and 8 February 1974; it told the story of Woomera. *Beating About The Bush* focused on the construction of the Sandy Blight Junction Road and parts of the Gary Junction Road, and was written from 21 November 1974 to 17 September 1975.

Each time a manuscript was completed, Len took it to Rigby. The Editor-in-Chief would simply flick through the pages and say 'we'll print this straight away'. Len remained very appreciative of Rigby's continuous willingness to keep publishing his every work. Indeed Rigby themselves first approached Len in September 1977 about the concept of extracting individual chapters from each of his five previous books, arranging them in chronological sequence, and calling the new book *The Best of Len Beadell*. As Rigby explained to Len, he had attracted such a following of dedicated readers that it was now Len's name they put on the front cover first, and the title came later.

Len initially had mixed feelings about the proposed new book. He still had one further book he wanted to write, which would detail the construction of the Gary Highway, the Talawana Track and the Gary Junction Road to Callawa. He also disliked the title 'Best of'. However, after further persuasive argument, Len agreed to Rigby's request, on the condition that the book be called *Outback Highways*. According to Len, he physically tore out chapters from each of his five books which he considered to be most representative of his work. Rigby accepted Len's selection of material. *Outback Highways* first appeared on the bookshelves on 21 November 1979.

As previously mentioned, Len was determined to write one final book. He knew in his own mind that he would never be completely satisfied unless the last part of his Outback story was told. However, by his own admission, Len found it difficult to become self-motivated and disciplined. In his own words: 'When

I started the books, I had my ears back and it was full on. But *End of an Era* became somewhat of a chore and I completed it under great duress. When I had some spare time, I was constantly finding excuses to do anything but write.' *End of an Era* was first published in 1983, after seven years of interrupted writing from October 1975 to August 1982.

There remained for many years one hidden jewel in Len Beadell's book-writing repertoire. Until recently, few people knew that Len wrote a book in 1967 which was never published. A complete manuscript, ready for the presses, lay tucked away in a cardboard box at his Salisbury home, collecting dust for almost 30 years. Entitled *Around The World in Eighty Delays*, it described a 5-month overseas holiday to America, Africa and Europe, which Len undertook from 1 June to 27 October 1959 as part of his accumulated long service leave at WRE. It is written with the same humorous flair which became the Beadell trademark in his series of books on Outback Australia. In many ways, the storyline closely resembles the exploits of a modern-day Crocodile Dundee, only 30 years ahead of Paul Hogan's time. After hearing of the manuscript's existence in mid-1997, Dr Richard Barnes from Corkwood Press approached Len's family about the possibility of publishing this work. *Around The World In Eighty Delays* first hit the bookshops in November 1997.

During the 1960-1970s, Len regularly wrote articles for *Missile*, a quarterly newsletter produced for workers at the Weapons Research Establishment. Two of these articles, which describe Len's overseas exploits in England and Paris during 1959, are reproduced here. They are similar to, but different from, corresponding chapters appearing in *Around The World in Eighty Delays. Been Invited to Redford Lately?* was first published in April-June 1965 issue of *Missile*. It describes Len's reunion with General Sir John Evetts and a visit to Redford Barracks, where Evetts' son was Commanding Officer. *Paris à la Beadell*, which appeared in the January-March 1966 edition of *Missile*, captures Len's attempts to come to grips with French language and culture. The latter has been edited and shortened from its original form.

Beryl Mazzacchi

The Len Beadell collection of books, showing the first edition of each title.

Been Invited to Redford Lately?

R EDFORD Barracks, Edinburgh, Scotland. Steeped in heavy
tradition; immersed in the strictest discipline; soaked in iron-
clad rules, regulations and ritual; saturated with ceremony. It's a
wonder half of its members don't go down with pleurisy every
winter. [I thought of them while in bed during my own recent
attack which gave rise to the 'germ' of the idea for this story].
They wear coloured rope, looped around their clavicles and
frayed at the ends to form tassels; their chests are covered with
medals and ornaments all of which have histories behind them;
they have toothbrush moustaches, great long swords hanging at
their sides from polished leather belts, and things called trews.
The latter are skin-tight trews – ah – trousers made from tartan
material, full length right down to the ground, and they force the
wearers to walk as if each leg was encased in a roll of lino. Then
to complete the picture, some even wear, above all things, a

monacle. When I saw these I thought they just had to be kidding. They are circular in shape, made of glass with a black edging, worn in the left eye, and attached to the jacket at the chest by a piece of black plumbob string long enough to give unrestricted movement of the neck. The ones who have them invariably say 'By Gad' at least once every 10 minutes and register surprise by raising the eyebrows sufficient to allow them to fall out; and this gave me a clue as to why they are mostly worn in the left eye. If they fall to the length of the string on the right side, they would almost certainly hit the handle of the sword and break.

I wondered how I looked to them when I walked into the Mess. Although I had put on my best desert boots and changed my belt for a barometer strap, I had a feeling that I was the one who was different. I still wore my watch pouch and pen knife on my belt as you never know when you might need to skin something; but, although it was all very practical, it didn't look like any uniform they had ever seen.

Redford is the home of the Royal Scots Fusiliers, I think. During 1959 they were undergoing some sort of an amalgamation with another mob, but I just can't think of who they were now; I don't even remember them being referred to as another mob, and very likely they weren't. But everyone was as pleased as fury with the operation. One thing I learned there, which I stored with my accumulation of useless information, was that a 'fusil' is a light musket like a cap gun, and fusiliers are the infantrymen who carry them. The fusil has gone out of date but, like many other things, they still retain the name.

It all started actually back in Tewkesbury, Gloucestershire, at the home of General Sir John Evetts, the father of the current Commanding Officer of Redford, Colonel Evetts. I suppose to be more precise it really began in North Terrace, Adelaide, in 1947 when I had a conference with the General concerning details of where might be a good place to open up some sort of a range for trying out rockets or something, out in the desert, a project which has now become slightly better known as Woomera. After that first meeting he used to occasionally call into our small survey camp at Woomera to see how things were getting along, before finally returning to England to furnish his reports. I knew him only from those relatively brief contacts.

The thing now was, would he remember me 12 years later and 12 000 miles removed as I drove up to his house in Gloucestershire? There had been a publication about a foot thick in London called *Who's Who* and I had discovered his address one day while flicking through it. You only needed a very small hydraulic jack to handle it. As I approached Sir John's house, I drove onto a gravel driveway through an open fence. Before I had time to switch off the engine, I heard a lusty 'Well bless my soul, if it's not Lennie Beadell,' and marvelled at his amazing memory. He bounded over and, after instructing me to park the car alongside the other two on the drive, began pounding me on the shoulder with one hand as he wrung my hand with the other. I replied to his first question as to what I was doing in England by saying that at the present minute I was having a rather rough time. I then managed to mumble something about not being sure whether he would remember me or not and was rewarded with an extra hard punch on the chest with 'Upon my word! As if anyone could forget ...' Perhaps it would be better if I didn't finish off the quote.

We went over to the group sitting at a rustic table on the lawn and was introduced firstly to Lady Evetts and then to the young man with military bearing who was his son, Colonel Evetts from Redford 'Ay what.' On learning that I was on a car trip around the UK, he immediately invited me to call into the barracks the moment I arrived in Edinburgh and meet the members of the Mess. It was then I was informed that he was the Commanding Officer of that establishment. His own small son who had been playing in the creek which ran through the grounds came over to the group at this point to meet 'The Australian.' His manners were perfect and he showed his interest by enquiring about the health of the kangaroos; whereupon I obtained a pencil and piece of paper and began to draw him some pictures of them and of the Aborigines with their spears. He was soon engrossed in my drawings and my stories, as were the General and Lady Evetts and the Colonel. As I told the young boy about the big aerodrome in Australia which was named 'Evetts Field' after his grandpa, I noticed Sir John proudly beaming out of the corner of my eye while, at the same time, endeavouring to appear nonchalant. He was obviously greatly attached to his grandson and anything helping the returning admiration from the boy caused him deep pleasure.

One afternoon, about a month after I'd negotiated the maze of one way traffic streets, the *Stop Do Not Enter* signs – and the police trying to enforce them all – I found myself in the shadow of Edinburgh Castle where I sought a telephone and was eventually connected to Redford Barracks. Sure enough, they had all heard of Colonel Evetts who was summoned to the 'phone. Directions were given and I was soon on my way to where he told me his officers would be waiting to welcome me to Scotland. After stopping in a paddock long enough to change into the barometer strap, I drove to where the guard had been instructed to allow me through and stopped at the huge grey-rock headquarters where the Colonel was on hand to show me into the inner sanctum.

It was as I was being ushered into the officer's lounge that I became aware of 'the atmosphere', and I knew straight away that one of us had to go. There were about 10 officers in all, dressed in trews and coloured rope, and I was introduced in turn to Lieutenant Ramrod, Captain Cutlass, Major Monacle and so on. They rose stiffly to their feet and acknowledged the greeting with an almost imperceptible inclination of the head, loaded with dignity and breeding. I suddenly hit upon the reason as to why they rose stiffly. It was those trews. When the introductions were completed, I decided that something would have to be done about 'the atmosphere', and quickly. So I went over to Captain Cutlass in order to examine more closely the hilt of his sword. I then remarked with just the right tone about how well they made things in 1066. A faint discreet titter rippled through the group which gave me hope, and soon I found that they were in fact a 'jolly decent bunch of chaps.' All except that is, Lieutenant Ramrod who, being the junior officer, felt he shouldn't relax too much in the presence of the Colonel. I thought what a victory it would be to cause the Lieutenant to thaw.

Suddenly the Colonel gave the order: 'Look here, would one of you chaps press the button for the orderly and his tray?' In a matter of milli-micro seconds, if there is such a unit of time, a Corporal appeared carrying a large silver tray and glided over to stand behind me. He was impeccably attired from his silky white face to his gleaming hob-nailed boots and I took a quick look to see if the Lieutenant was still there. Being the guest, I was asked first what I'd like to drink. So I turned around to face the Corporal and I told him that I would like to have a cup of cocoa. There was a dead silence for three seconds broken by the Major saying 'By Gad', as his monacle fell out and became hooked in the rope. The Corporal controlled himself magnificently and there was nothing more than a slight movement of the tray and a flicker of his eyelashes. Best of all, the lips of the Lieutenant were at last curved geometrically into a smile. Very small and sedate but nevertheless a smile! The unfortunate NCO said: 'Certainly Sir' and, after everyone then asked for cocoa, he disappeared in a hurry to a place where he could burst with laughter in private.

'Mug of cocoa ...'

Everyone who visits Redford has to view their silver. It's kept on shelves in a dark cellar and very traditional, shaped into cups, trays, vases, and carved, engraved and etched. It's been there for donkey's years. I had the full history of each piece explained as it was reverently handed to me bit by bit for inspection. During a lull in the proceedings Major Monacle drew me aside and whispered: 'I say, awfully sorry to do this to you old boy but I

Len, the author, signing books at yet another launch, July 1989.

can't do a thing about it.' He was nearly crying on my shoulder by the time it was over, but it really was quite interesting.

I mentioned that I had a pre-arranged visit to the theodolite factory in York organised for the following day, and all the officers feverishly discussed how I could best be there on time as it was some 100 miles away. I was to leave my car at the barracks and be taken to the railway station in one of their staff cars. As soon as I got back I was to ring again, whereupon a car would come to return me to my own vehicle. They were a helpful and wonderful 'bunch of chaps' all right, once you got through to them, and I hoped that the next visitor from Australia would find it easier going. I often wondered how that person got on. The driver of the staff car would have been equally as jolly as the rest of them but there was not time between the barracks and the station to find out anything more than the fact that the only word of English he seemed to know was 'Sir.'

Later at the Farnborough Air Show I again met General Sir John at his stand selling aeroplane propellers – just where he said he would be. He had obviously heard of my visit to Redford. He was pleased as punch at the whole thing and asked me first hand what I thought of Redford. I could quite truthfully tell him that they can sure make the nicest cocoa.

Paris à la Beadell

WHILE circling over Paris on the short flight from London, I wondered what it would be like on the ground and searched from the plane window for that Eiffel Tower I'd heard so much about. I hoped that the tower would not damage the underside of the Super Constellation if we got too close to it, being so sharp and everything. The tempo started immediately upon landing and kept up the same furious pace throughout my stay in Paris. While waiting in the terminal building I noticed that everyone seemed in such a state of impatience that they just couldn't sit still – and most couldn't even sit, but instead stormed back and forth quite oblivious to each other while keeping up an incessant muttering to themselves with heads inclined showing expressions in tune with their thoughts.

I rode to the hôtel d'Iéna in a taxi – accompanied by a smell of burning rubber and the screech of tyres ringing in my ears. I took up my little bag containing my other shirt, desert boots, shorts and watch pouch and shakily entered the lobby. I hadn't had a chance to wear these since leaving Oodnadatta as I thought they'd look a bit out of place on Broadway or in Madame Tussaud's waxworks museum. At the desk I was relieved to see my name on their register as a result of the careful pre-planning by the airlines. I was immediately set upon by two bellhops, and four hangers-on who accompanied me to my room. One carried my little bag while the other opened doors and pushed the buttons on the lift. When we got to my room the other four opened windows, pulled back the bed covers, opened my bag and neatly laid out my desert boots on the floor. The fact that they each left with a share of my francs was proof that they had out shuffled me.

It was so hot that firstly I wanted to have a shower before setting out to see my number one sight. No! Wrong. I meant 'La Tour Eiffel', and not the Folies. There didn't seem to be a shower in the room or for that matter even a tap or dish, let alone a towel or soap which would have been useless under the circumstances anyway. There was a phone though so I rang the office and this was my first clash with the language here, of which I knew nothing. After listening to what sounded like a corroboree in several different voices, some English came out of the earpiece asking what it was I wanted. Relieved, I asked where I could get a bath as I'd already peered along all the corridors for some signs of a community pool. The voice said it would be arranged immediately and put the extra 500 francs involved on my bill. This looked like being quite an expensive visit until I worked out on my cardboard slide rule that this was only a few bob after all.

In a very few seconds, at least seven ladies were there at my door carrying half a dozen towels (one for your face, one for your ears, another for your hands and a separate one for feet, etc. – I think), an array of chemicals, a bottle of small stones and someone had even thought to bring a lump of soap. Thinking they would give them all to me and tell me where the water was, I held out my arms hoping I was strong enough to carry it all on my own, only to see them start hiking off down the passageway indicating for me to follow. I saw them turn into a small niche in the wall and got there just in time to see the last one disappearing through a door. No wonder I hadn't noticed the bathroom I thought, as I ran behind, almost out of breath trying to keep up. I got into the room, just before the door slammed in my face, to see them rushing around the bath tub laying out all their apparatus. Expecting them to leave me to it, a feeling bordering on panic swept over me when one turned on the water, as the others emptied in the chemicals followed by the contents of the bottle of stones. If only I could have conversed with them as they issued a rapid hail of orders to each other in French – it would have helped, but still they stayed. The room smelt worse than the burning rubber in the taxi as the chemicals hit the hot water, and I thought how rough it was going to be in the tub sitting on the stones. Then just as I was about to say some bright remark such as 'now look here ladies, but hasn't this gone quite far enough,' they trooped out and left me to have what had started out to be originally only just a bit of a clean-up. If everyone had to go through this each time they needed a wash in Paris, then I could see some truth in what I'd heard ...

Here at last was the time to start wearing khaki shorts with desert boots again as it was hotter than ever. It would be easier climbing about the Eiffel Tower anyway. I planned to go down to have some dinner first at Place d'Iéna, then get a map from the office, upon which I could mark a cross to indicate where I was living in order to be able to get home after each day's expedition. The uproar brought on by the appearance of the shorts commenced on my way through the lobby as they apparently had never seen anyone over ten years old in them.

At Place d'Iéna the menu meant nothing to me as did the talk from the waiters, until a simple solution presented itself to me. I merely took out my pen and on a paper napkin sketched a string of sausages with a ring around four of them, and a chook sitting on two large eggs. They laughed until their eyes filled with mineral water tears indicating with wild gestures that NOW they knew what I wanted, and went off to the kitchen complete with the napkin. I had thought of putting the string of sausages trailing from the mouth of a poodle running down the street with an angry butcher carrying a meat cleaver in hot pursuit, but thinking of the stories of frog's legs and snails, thought I might get boiled dog instead.

After consulting my map, I found the Eiffel Tower was within easy walking distance of where I was living. So I hurried off with my camera at the ready. Soon it was easy to see, rearing up into the sky resembling an oversized deck quoits peg, and nestling on the banks of a good big creek which they called the Seine according to my plan. The next thing was to try and get to the top somehow, for it was a bright sunny day and I wanted to take some of my very own pictures of Paris. Just as I was wondering how to go about it I saw a large drawing of the tower on a sign on one of the supports with three arrows pointing horizontally at it; one indicating the first floor level, the next the second, and the third pointing to the top. These had 100 francs, 200 francs and 500 francs labelled on them respectively. I immediately thought to myself that here it costs as much to reach the top of the Eiffel Tower as it does to have a bath. There was an elevator running on rails through one of the legs of the structure with three stages and, armed with my 500 franc coupon, I finished up on the journey skywards. The network of steel narrowed until there didn't seem enough around the cage to support it. As we neared the 900-foot mark I remember opening my eyes and then looking down. I shuddered five months later, as I thought again of that view when I read that a lady had leapt off the tower from there. I wondered how they knew it was a lady after she landed. These French people can tell, I suppose.

When I returned to earth some minutes later, I was on my way to what looked to be one of the main streets in Paris, namely one called the Avenue des Champs Elysées.

When I got to a thing called the Arc de Triomphe I noticed someone had a camp fire going under it, but an English-speaking visitor told me that it never went out and was used as a symbol and not for cooking. Walking down the Champs Elysées I noticed everyone would look right on past anyone wearing a scarlet sheet dragging along the ground, and would not even see another wearing her hair heaped up two feet high and held in place with turkey feathers; but they all stopped to stare at me in my shorts and desert boots. I started to wonder just who was different after all. Maybe it was me. It was a disturbing thought. Anyway, I fixed it all up by simply pushing down my socks made by my aunt in Sydney, and no one took any notice again.

The next day I went to the Louvre Museum to see the Mona Lisa. I paid to get into the door of the Louvre and again to get past the second door. Then they wanted some more francs to get into the wing containing jolly old Mona Lisa. I gave it up when I saw another door with a man and a bag of tickets at it with another beyond that. No wonder Lisa was a moaner.

At the statue of Jeanne d'Arc, I asked a gendarme how I could get to Pigalle and he impatiently waved me away with a lump of wood he was carrying. I had to then rely upon my map until I saw a hole in the street labelled 'Métro.' It resembled a similar hole in Sydney I'd seen where you went to get a train, so I thought I'd give it a try and soon came to a cage where there was a fella selling more tickets. I said Pigalle, and he threw a card at me and I threw some francs right back. This was the treatment he could understand. I arrived at the right train by showing everyone my drawing of a windmill. It was all I could think of as I'd heard the Moulin Rouge was also there. At a later stop I saw the word Pigalle up on a sign, but as I ambled along to the door, the train started off again. You have to move quicker here than in Oodnadatta.

Finally I raced off the return train and was at last free to try and get back to the surface of the earth. Everyone of the tunnels leading off the platform went to some place they called 'Sortie' but I wanted to go to Pigalle. It must have been quite an important place because, after twenty minutes of walking, every tunnel led to Sortie. So not wanting to come to a miserable end perishing in a Paris rabbit warren after surviving the Gibson Desert, I realised I'd just have to go there. So I followed the sign. In a minute I was surfacing as it were and by now it had become almost dusk. I checked on the signs with another English tourist, and found that the French word for exit was *sortie*.

Well this was the famous Pigalle at last. It wasn't long before I came to a most uninviting-looking establishment with the words Folies Bergères written in lights over it. I think I must have been at the back door because I was sure I'd heard of this place somewhere and imagined it to be nice on the outside. They would not let people dressed in khaki shorts and penknife pouch inside, not that I tried. Then as I went along a dimly lit alley, I noticed a man walking towards me. This was another thing which would not normally cause comment, but in this case you just couldn't help noticing him, what with his shoulders four feet wide and his black arms hanging down to his knees like that orang-utan in the Adelaide Zoo. His skin was black, as were his clothes and heavy sun-glasses, and he seemed to all but fill the whole alley. I edged past him on what was left of the sidewalk and thought I was glad I'd never have to tangle with him. But as I walked away I became aware that he had turned around somehow in that space and was retracing his steps along behind me. The hairs on my neck crawled as I listened to his feet paddling surprisingly softly along near me so I immediately turned as he had done and walked past him once more. This seemed to confuse him and he stopped with his hairy arms hanging loosely and his huge jaw sagging, rather like the expression worn by a giddy ape. I've never seen a giddy ape but you probably see what I mean. Apparently this was not what I was supposed to do in his book of rules, which would have stated that I should keep on walking until he could fell me with one swipe of his paw leaving me to lie bleeding in a gutter minus my British passport. I had been told that our passports brought good prices in the continental underworld, so I had left mine poked into a loose flap in the torn floral wallpaper in my hotel room.

I eventually got to the 'big windmill' after beating my way past half a dozen furtive little characters trying to sell me some postcards. I suddenly thought that I didn't have any idea where I was after that train trip in the Métro. So I decided to try and go home on foot because it was after midnight and I didn't feel confident enough to face the Sortie tunnels again so soon.

I must have hiked ten more miles without knowing it as it was now four o'clock in the morning as I emerged out onto the Champs Elysées which would take me to the Arc de Triomphe and eventually to the good old Avenue d'Iéna. That is if I turned south.

After hurrying through the doorway of Nôtre Dame and visiting the Bastille the next day, I was glad the time had came to go to the next place in my book of airline tickets.

I had at least left something behind me in Paris. All those sketches I had done on the paper napkins had all been pinned in a neat line in the kitchen of the Place d'Iéna!

END NOTES

Len's Overseas Itinerary, 1959

1 June	Leave Adelaide for San Francisco, via Sydney and Honolulu
4-5 June	San Francisco
6-9 June	Las Vegas
10 June	Grand Canyon
12 June	Chicago
13-14 June	Washington
15 June	New York
16-19 June	Boston
21-24 June	New York
25 June	Fly to London
1-3 July	Dover
4-11 July	London
12-20 July	Brighton, Leicester, Banbury Cross
21 July	Drive to Aldermaston to see Sir William Penney
22-28 July	Stay with Sir William Penney
9-14 August	Ireland
15 August	
-1 September	Touring English and Scottish countryside and Edinburgh
2-18 September	London
19 September	Fly to Paris
20 September	
-6 October	Tour around Europe; Switzerland, Italy, Austria, Greece
7 October	Fly to Nairobi
7-11 October	Tour around Africa
15 October	Fly to Bombay
21-26 October	Singapore
29 October	Arrive Sydney

Around The World in Eighty Delays was written by Len between 11 January and 13 July 1967. The final typed version was completed on 18 October 1967. Rigby informed Len that they would not be publishing the manuscript in November 1967.

Chapter 10

$\mathcal{T}$HE CONSUMMATE TOUR GUIDE

L EN BEADELL'S work in opening up the Western Deserts of
Australia officially concluded in 1963, yet his heart and spirit
remained with the Outback. Len's whirlwind desert trip
with Donald Thomson in 1965 only served to reinforce his desire
to return as often as he could to the country he loved so
passionately.

On 18 October 1967 Len first met Rex Ellis, who two years
earlier had begun to operate commercial Adelaide-based safaris to
the Birdsville and Nullarbor Plain regions. Rex had heard of Len's
exploits in the Western Deserts and was keen to take tourists into
this area. He rang Len and arranged to visit his Salisbury home.
Rex asked Len if he would be interested in acting as guest
narrator/guide on a commercial trip to the Gibson Desert, where
he could tell the passengers about his historic road-making feats
– in person and out there in the desert! Len accepted Rex's offer
without hesitation because he was keen to revisit the area and the
trip would enable him to gather further practical field information
for *Bush Bashers*.

So began a 25-year association between Len and a series of
well-known Outback safari tour operators, namely Rex, Dick Lang
(South Australia), Peter Vernon (Victoria) and Russell Guest
(Victoria). Although beginning as a business enterprise, Len's
relationship with each operator quickly developed into one of
long-term friendship and mutual respect. Rex, Dick and Peter
relate some of their experiences with Lenny.

Rex Ellis

A LTHOUGH their initial meeting took place late in 1967, it was
not until July 1969 that Rex's first desert safari with Len

141

Len shares a light-hearted moment with fellow entertainer Rolf Harris at Ayers Rock in 1969.

became a reality. Their three-week journey in a converted International AB120 van took them from Adelaide to Alice Springs, and onto Ayers Rock, Docker River, Giles, Warburton, Mt Beadell, Carnegie, Laverton, Kalgoorlie and Rawlinna, before returning to Adelaide via the Eyre Highway. While at Ayers Rock, Len met well-known entertainer Rolf Harris (who was filming for his television series *Walkabout*), Harry Butler, and Vincent and Carol Serventy.

Rex and Len were back in the desert for a second safari from 2-26 July 1971. They initially travelled via Alice Springs, Ayers Rock and Docker River to the Sandy Blight Junction Road, where a major mechanical breakdown near Mt Leisler forced them to abandon their trailer and tow their damaged vehicle back to Alice. Two days of frantic repairs to the vehicle were necessary before the safari headed westward again; this time they travelled the Gunbarrel Highway past the Rawlinson Range to Warburton, drove the entire length of the Connie Sue Highway to Rawlinna, and returned home via the Eyre Highway.

Rex learnt much about Len's character from the many incidents that occurred during the course of these two trips. He reflects on some of these events.

I REALLY valued the time I spent with Len. He showed me places I thought I would never have the opportunity to visit.

His rapport with people was something really special. He always had time to talk to those who wanted to hear his stories and willingly gave so much of himself, yet he also made time to listen to others. He was incredibly patient and tolerant with people. I'll give you some examples.

During our first trip, we stayed overnight in Alice Springs. Len took the opportunity to renew acquaintances with his old trucking mate and member of the Gunbarrel Road Construction Party, Frank Quinn. Len rolled out his swag in Quinny's yard amongst 'a heap of old car bodies' and I listened intently as the two mates reminisced the night away. It was interesting to observe the respect and intensely close friendship they shared with each other.

Len was always warmly welcomed in Aboriginal settlements we

Mark Sheppard

Len never tired of relating stories about the bush he loved so much.

visited. On both occasions we called into Docker River, Aboriginal people gathered enthusiastically to greet him. They all remembered him from his road-building days and obviously held him in high esteem. The children in particular would flock around him and grab him by the leg. It was like a long-lost relative had come home to see them.

On returning to Adelaide across the Nullarbor during our first trip, we called into Gunadorah Station, east of Rawlinna. I introduced Len to Colvin (Collie) Day, the station owner, who was also an old mate of mine. Len and Collie struck an immediate rapport. Len really enjoyed meeting the battlers of the bush, the contemporary pioneers if you like. It didn't matter how well-off or how poor a person was, Len treated everyone as his equal.

While discussing that first trip, I recall the night we arrived in Kalgoorlie. One of my passengers, who was a keen 'Lion', asked Len if he would be interested in attending the Lions Club meeting that night. Len was initially hesitant because he said he didn't have any suitable clothes. He was eventually dragged along in his grey coat and shorts, with socks pulled up over his boots. Len took the club by storm and ended up talking for half the night. It was an evening of fun and laughter the locals have never forgotten. Len had an incredible gift of being able to walk into a room of complete strangers and make them immediately feel that they had known him for most of their lives.

One of the passengers on our second desert trip in 1971 was an American named Roger A.C. Stephens. The words 'Roger A.C. Stephens, Boston, Massachusetts, Destination – The World' were emblazoned across his backpack. He talked as though he had a football in his throat but, at the same time, he had an insatiable appetite for detail and a photographic memory. Most of the other passengers found him difficult to get on with. He latched on to Len, followed him everywhere and badgered him constantly for more information and fine detail about the country. I regularly asked Len whether he wanted me to divert Roger away from him for a while, but Len was in fact quite fascinated and intrigued by his personality. He was incredibly tolerant, even to someone who was infuriating to others.

Len also had a wicked sense of humour and a mischievous nature, as evidenced by the following story, which involved our friend Roger Stephens.

We were driving along the dirt road south of Alice. As driver, I was always listening for sounds which might indicate mechanical trouble. Suddenly I heard a noise, something like 'pfewt'. A flat tyre, I thought. I stopped the vehicle and checked the tyres. There were no flats. I didn't say anything to the passengers and kept driving. Suddenly I heard 'pfewt' again. Once more I brought the vehicle to a halt and examined the wheels; same result, no punctures. After the fourth enforced stop, I was suspicious. I looked in the rear vision mirror after we had driven through deep bulldust to see Roger blowing some of the dust off his sleeve with a 'pfewt' sound. Len almost broke down with laughter. He had known the source of the noise all along and didn't tell me; instead he played along with the joke!

There were many other aspects of Len's character which I admired. He had a steely determination not to be beaten by unforseen circumstances and a resolve that no situation was impossible.

After leaving Ayers Rock on our '69 desert trip, I turned the International van westwards along 'that little wheel track that used to be the road to Docker River.' It wasn't long before the van's roofrack, laden down with swags and assorted material, came tumbling to earth. It was simply not repairable without a good welder, yet Len was determined that something could be done to fix it. I literally had to drag him away from the rack, before finally leaving it suspended from a nearby mulga tree.

A broken piston in the Land Rover caused the abandonment of our second expedition along the Sandy Blight Junction Road. We were 500 kilometres from Alice Springs and at the time I wished I was doing anything else for a living but this. It was a 'terminal situation', yet Len spent the next day and a half exhausting ways and means by which something could be salvaged from the situation. He never gave up.

Being the last of the true Australian explorers himself, Len was fascinated by the exploratory feats of others. Our date of arrival at Kalgoorlie in 1969 coincided with Neil Armstrong stepping onto the surface of the moon. I'd never seen Len so excited and enthralled as he was with this feat of human endeavour.

In talking with Len about his own road-building achievements, I always sensed that he was wary of bureaucracy and had deliberately made an artform out of 'being out of control.' He realised with his work that he was really 'in the box seat' to get whatever he wanted and whenever he wanted it. There was no other person who could have bettered Len at his job. He literally had the bureaucrats 'snookered' when he said he wanted a new vehicle or piece of equipment, or when he said a particular task may take another six weeks knowing all the while it may require only 10 minutes work. Officialdom was powerless to over-ride him, and he played it to the hilt.

Dick Lang

D ICK Lang is the former director of the well-known Adelaide-based company Desert-Trek Australia, which specialised in four-wheel drive safaris commencing in the 1960s. More recently Dick has taken his interest in nature-based tours literally to the air, as director of Dick Lang's Desert-Air Safaris. Dick first met Len in 1970 when he sought his advice on travelling into the Gibson Desert. The pair spent countless hours together in the loungeroom of Len's home, pouring over maps, detailing the country and discussing places to visit. One of Dick's most treasured possessions is an old survey sheet of the Gibson Desert, onto which Len meticulously marked the route of his Gunbarrel Highway. As time progressed Len and 'Desert Dick', as the latter became affectionately known, forged a deep long-term friendship based on mutual respect for each other and their shared love of the Australian bush. In fact, Len coined a special term for their friendship, namely 'MAS' which stood for 'Mutual Admiration Society.' The abbreviation became a continuing source of amusement and laughter between the pair.

Len first took on the role of guest narrator with Dick's commercial safaris in 1984. He continued to work with Dick in

Courtesy, Dick Lang

Len and his good mate, Dick Lang, near the base of Mt Beadell in the Gibson Desert.

Passengers on the second leg of Dick Lang's safari commemorating the 30th Anniversary of the completion of the Gunbarrel Highway experienced the parkland-like appearance of the western end of the Anne Beadell Highway.

Mark Shephard

this capacity for the next seven consecutive years. Desert-Trek's comprehensive advertising campaign promoting Len as guest tour operator complemented Len's already high level of popularity achieved through his lectures and books.

Len's initial safari with Desert-Trek, from 23 June to 8 July 1984, travelled the following route: Adelaide to Ayers Rock, Docker River and Giles, then along the Gunbarrel Highway to Warburton and Carnegie, onto Laverton, Coolgardie and Norseman, and then back to Adelaide via the Eyre Highway. The Gunbarrel Highway was again the centrepiece of their safari in June the following year.

Len's daughter Connie accompanied the pair on their April 1986 tour, which took in the Gunbarrel Highway but returned to Adelaide from Laverton via Neale Junction, Rawlinna and Cocklebiddy. Two tours were conducted during 1987, in April and September; each followed a similar route to the previous year but concluded with a train journey from Rawlinna to Adelaide. Len celebrated his 64th birthday at Ayers Rock during the first tour, a tradition which continued on later April safaris. When Anzac Day coincided with a Desert-Trek expedition, Len would also conduct a short service.

The year 1988 marked the 30th Anniversary of the completion of the Gunbarrel Highway and Dick organised a special tour to commemorate this feat. Len and his wife Anne were special guests of the tour which was conducted in two legs. The first followed part of the Gunbarrel Highway through the Gibson Desert. A celebratory 30th Anniversary cake was cut after the party's arrival at Carnegie. Each passenger was given a certificate featuring an illustration which was hand-drawn by Len. The tour then traversed the western Great Victoria Desert along both the Anne Beadell and Connie Sue Highways before concluding at Rawlinna. A further party of tourists flew in to join the expedition at the lonely railway siding. The second leg of the trip continued north along the Connie Sue Highway to Neale Junction and then east along the Anne Beadell Highway to Coober Pedy. Dick drove a large four-wheel drive bus to take passengers on the tour.

In August 1988 Connie again joined Len on another Dick Lang

tour which followed the same route as the trip earlier that year across the Gibson and Great Victoria Deserts. Phil Sexton and Steve Holden accompanied the tour in its early stages to undertake some promotional filming for a new video about Len's desert exploits, to be called *Too Long In The Bush*. Len met the Governor of South Australia, Sir Donald Dunstan, and his wife at Giles during the safari.

Three months after completing this trip, Dick was diagnosed with a rare form of leukaemia. He spent many long months undergoing radical treatment at the Royal Adelaide Hospital. In a remarkable testament to his courage and determination, Dick beat the disease and remains in good health today while continuing to run his air-based safari company.

Dick provides a personal perspective on Len's character and their valued friendship.

WHILE the exploits of Len Beadell in Central and Western Australia are well-known and revered, perhaps not quite so well documented is the very private and personal side of his life.

During my years as a tour operator (both land and air), I have met, travelled and had to live with hundreds of people, often in trying and very difficult circumstances. For reasons of professional and personal survival, I have had to become a very astute and accurate judge of character. I have never met nor feel that I am likely to ever meet again anyone who was so honest, charming and accommodating as Len Beadell.

When faced with the adulation of almost every Outback traveller and person who was interested in the Australian bush, Len remained refreshingly humble and personable. I frequently heard people ask of him: 'Don't you feel proud to have made the roads across Australia?' to which Len always replied: 'No, I don't feel proud, rather I feel it was a privilege that I was allowed to do the work I did.' This simple statement sums up his philosophy about his early exploration and surveying.

In the 25 years that I knew Len, I never heard him say a cross word about anyone, nor ever be uncharitable in thought or deed. Len was always the same – morning or night. He had a friendly

Mark Shephard

*Len and a passenger sign the visitor's book at Vokes Hill Corner in the
Great Victoria Desert.*

and warm attitude to everyone he met, whether they were
passengers on our desert safaris or interested people who would
stream to his Salisbury home to talk to him. I've known hundreds
of people who are forever grateful for the time and conversation
he so happily gave to them. I am also particularly appreciative of
how close Len became to my eldest son, Lachlan.

When I suffered from leukaemia in 1988, Len visited me
regularly in hospital and at home. I treasure the cards he drew to
jolly up my spirits. We always had a really good laugh together
and would reminisce over so many matters that the visits together
were fun.

Later I was to visit him in hospital and at his home during his
own recovery from a heart operation. Many times he would laugh
and ask me to stop telling stories because his surgery was still
healing and the laughter hurt him. But on the serious side, we
also confided closely in each other in recent years.

Looking back again on our desert safari days, it did not matter
how difficult the weather, the roads or the circumstances became,

Len would remain calm and unruffled. If he was able to offer advice on a particular situation or subject he would cautiously suggest something, so that it did not interfere.

There were many memorable moments.

On one trip across the Gunbarrel early in the 1980s, Len told people in our group how he filled 44-gallon (200-litre) petrol drums with sand and rock, then drilled holes in the drums to attach his signs at road junctions. When pressed, he admitted that he drilled these holes using bullets fired from his .38 Service Revolver.

Thereafter for many years I would talk to him about his 'drill.' Finally in 1991, on my 50th birthday, Len gave me the original framed drawing used in his book *End of an Era* showing him using his pistol on a petrol drum. To my great pleasure not long after, Len gave me his actual 'defused drill.' Len was not a person who gave away his possessions lightly, and so I treasured this gift.

Over the years I felt that I had acquired a good bit of bush sense, but whenever we came to a road junction or to a natural feature where our opinions differed, I learned to listen carefully to Len. Sometimes though, Len was not always correct. This led to he and I placing Mt Woodroffe in the Musgrave Ranges (in

north-west South Australia) at many different locations over the years. He satirised this in the drawing and commentary he wrote on the fly leaf of my personal copy of *Still in the Bush*: 'To Desert-Dick, together we were the only ones who could move the location of Mt Woodroffe on every trip we made, depending on who pointed it out first.'

Len's favourite campfire story related to the Russian satellite Sputnik, which was launched into space in the early 1960s. He used to tell people how it circled the world emitting a 'beep' sound. He would say to them that it went over Australia 'beep, beep, beep', then later over England 'beep, beep, beep' and then over America 'ha, ha, ha' ... His audience loved it.

Len also liked the story about the new winch he was given for his Land Rover. He thought it was one of the most practical gadgets he had ever seen. Soon enough, he was out in the bush and thoroughly bogged. He unravelled the winch cable and set about getting it working. Later, someone asked: 'How did you find the winch?' Len replied: 'It was excellent. It pulled out every mulga tree within 300 yards of where I was bogged!'

As Len and I sat together at the front of our safari vehicle, clocking up thousands upon thousands of kilometres of desert travel, we would often say to each other: 'Have you heard the joke about the Sputnik?' or 'have you heard the one about the dingo?' and so on. In the end Len and I decided, for the sake of expediency, that we'd tell our jokes by numbers. And so Len would say: 'Do you remember number 5?' I'd reply: 'Yes what a tremendous joke that is!' We'd then proceed to laugh our heads off at 'number 5.' This type of banter would carry on all the way down the Gunbarrel Highway as we shuddered (sorry, rode smoothly!) along the road. On one trip, this activity simply got too much for one of the passengers (Stephen). He leaned forward and asked Len what was going on. Len told him about our 'joke by number' system. Stephen said he would like to join in. Len replied: 'Be my guest. Tell a joke.' So Stephen then said: 'Number 14!' Len and I remained deadly silent. A puzzled Stephen enquired: 'Have you heard that one before?' To which Len quipped: 'No, but it was the terrible way you told it!'

Peter Vernon

P ETER Vernon, qualified mechanical engineer and current director of Victorian-based business Western Desert Wanderers, has been a friend of the Beadell family for the past 15 years.

Peter first learned of Len's road-building exploits following an impromptu conversation with a desert traveller at an Alice Springs caravan park in January 1980. The conversation left Peter totally spellbound by Len's accomplishments and he and his travelling companions were immediately compelled to head for the Gunbarrel Highway, despite the extreme midsummer heat, dust and flies. En route, a visit to the Giles Weather Station and discussions with the weather crew convinced Peter that Len Beadell was not only a superb bushman, explorer, surveyor and supervisor of desert road construction, but also a successful author, cartoonist and public speaker. After traversing the western section of the Gunbarrel Highway and witnessing the spectacular scenery of the Gibson Desert, Peter returned to Melbourne and feverishly read all of Len's books.

In 1982 Peter, by now a true Beadell disciple, decided to contact Len to find out more first-hand information about some of his other desert roads. Peter had a real desire and passion to travel to remote areas of the Outback and to attempt to relocate historic sites of early explorers; Len's roads provided the means by which Peter could realise his dreams. Finding Len in Adelaide proved easy, as there was only one Beadell in the metropolitan phonebook. However, Peter never made that initial phone call, dialling all but the last digit before putting the phone down. He considered that the chances of someone as 'important as Len' wanting to talk to him would be remote. Instead he wrote a letter to Len and was both surprised and excited when Len promptly replied, inviting Peter to drop in to his home and discuss his travel plans over maps.

A visit to the Beadells was immediately arranged and discussions about deserts went on late into the night. Peter takes up the story:

*Len greets Peter Vernon near the completion of Peter's run along the full length
of the Gunbarrel Highway in March/April 1986.*

*Len's wedding present to Peter and Helen Vernon; it is the last illustration ever
drawn by Len.*

T HIS was the beginning of a solid friendship and a long-term association with Australian deserts that has dramatically changed my life. I couldn't believe how willing Len was to part with the information and knowledge he had acquired. It was clear to me that Len had an exceptional memory for detail about the Australian bush. Len and I kept in regular contact over the next few years, exchanging trip notes and discussing various aspects of the Western Deserts.

In April 1985 I decided to attempt to run the full length of the Gunbarrel Highway from east to west, some 1 350 kilometres. I dedicated the run to Len, for the help he had given me and for the contribution he had made to opening up inland Australia. Despite months of training and preparation, I was forced to abandon my attempt at the 300-kilometre mark after dislocating an ankle and tearing ligaments in both legs due to the corrugated road surface. Len, Anne and daughter Jacqui had intended to meet me at Carnegie Station, the planned finishing point of the run. After hearing the news that I had been injured early in my attempt, the Beadells travelled from Adelaide to meet me in the desert. We spent three days together slowly driving the Gunbarrel from Giles to Jackie Junction. Len showed me important landmarks, pointed out interesting trees and plants, and retold many of the stories described in his books. These few days spent with Len and members of his family remain one of my most treasured experiences.

In March 1986 I made a second (and successful) attempt to run the Gunbarrel Highway, this time from west to east. I arrived wearily at Victory Downs homestead on 6 April, 23 days after leaving Carnegie. Len, Anne and daughter Connie made another whirlwind trip from Adelaide to meet me and Richard Mason, my sole support, near the finish of the run.

Later that year I established a new business, Breakaway Safaris, which specialised in guided desert tours. Len was only too keen to help out with my new venture. We called into Len's Salisbury home each time I brought a tour party through Adelaide. Len would willingly give the group an informal lecture and a solid briefing about the country through which we would be travelling.

He always made time to personally autograph copies of his books. These visits to the Beadell home ensured the tours inevitably departed on a good note.

Len later offered to come along on some of my desert expeditions as official tour guide. Our first trip together took place during October 1988. We travelled the Anne Beadell and Gunbarrel Highways. A core group of people from that trip are still coming away with me on desert safaris, nearly 10 years later. Len was just so comfortable interacting with people from all backgrounds and walks of life. Storytelling around the campfire was one of his specialities. He loved giving informal talks about his exploring and surveying work, or more specific topics such as taking astrofixes, desert dentistry, or some of his more ingenious improvisations as a bush mechanic. Family stories also featured highly, particularly one relating to an orchestra performance in which daughter Connie was playing the violin. Len was very tired after a heavy programme of lectures and desert trips and, during a lull in the performance, he happened to nod off. But when the orchestra reached a crescendo shortly after, Len launched out of his seat and shouted: 'What's happened? What's going on?' much to the embarrassment of those seated around him!

Len continued to act as tour guide on several more expeditions over the next five years. In September 1989, Len and I took a small group into the northern and eastern Great Victoria Desert. We located a long-abandoned camp near Emu Claypan which had been used temporarily by scientists involved in the British Nuclear Testing Program. We also revisited the 300-mile point along the centreline of fire of the Woomera Rocket Range. For Len, it was a great thrill to relive some old, yet treasured, memories.

In 1990, I changed the name of my business to Western Desert Wanderers. Len and I were both disappointed when torrential rain throughout the Outback forced the cancellation of an intended trip that year. In April 1991 we were back in the Great Victoria Desert with another tour group. We celebrated Len's 68th birthday in the mulga with a cake fashioned in the shape of a centreline survey peg site. During this trip we navigated with the use of a hand-held instrument known as a Global Positioning

System (GPS). This new electronic device could literally do in seconds what would have taken Len hours of painstaking work with his trusted theodolite.

Len was philosophical about technological advance and was the first to acknowledge that 'high tech stuff', as he called it, had its place in modern society ... like the time we were at the Beadell home in Salisbury and the subject of desert birds, in particular the crested bellbird, was raised. Len was keen to demonstrate the unique call of this unusual bird, which he called the morse-code bird. He began to press all sorts of buttons on the control panel of Anne's microwave oven to produce a series of beeps and tones which mimicked the bird's call. Anne soon terminated this activity, convinced that her oven was about to blow up or, at least, never work properly again!

In April 1993, Len celebrated his 70th birthday with a dinner and gathering of friends at Trinity College in Adelaide, where daughter Jacqui was a teacher. The night was full of storytelling and reminiscing about Len's past achievements. The unflappable Len took the official 'business side' of the function in his stride, but I'm sure he would have been more comfortable in his khaki shorts and hob-nailed boots out in the mulga and sandhills.

During the evening I met Doug Stoneham, the bulldozer driver with the Gunbarrel Road Construction Party. I had a desert tour departing for the Great Victoria Desert shortly thereafter and invited Doug to accompany Len as tour guide. The pair complemented each other perfectly. At Vokes Hill Corner, Len presented my contract driver Patrick Kenny with a certificate incorporating a trademark Beadell illustration; the certificate acknowledged the fact that Patrick had driven over all of Len's Outback roads, yet he had never owned a four-wheel-drive himself!

The next morning while vehicles were being packed, I sent various passengers off for a leisurely walk. Len and Doug were pointing out things of interest along the track and, as usual, reliving their roadmaking days. One of the passengers, Helen Maskell, spotted a brass cap about the size of a fifty cent piece. She had unknowingly found the cap of a pistol flare gun which

Len used during his road-making days to guide Doug on the 'dozer through thick scrub. This is now a most prized possession of the Vernon family.

Later during the tour, we travelled to Dingo Claypan and the 300-mile centreline peg, where we positioned a new ironbark post and brass plate next to the original partly-rotted mulga post. Len was really pleased, as he always took every opportunity to undertake meticulous restoration work on all his signposts and markers throughout his network of Outback roads.

I married Helen Maskell three years later. Len had been one of the first people I invited to the wedding, which was held at Dingo Claypan in the Great Victoria Desert on 13 April 1996. Len gave us a very special wedding gift – a large watercolour illustration depicting my run across the Gunbarrel Highway, with Helen assisting and holding an oversized can of Coca-Cola as refreshment. This gift was received from Len in hospital only a week before he died ... Len was truly an exceptional friend and will forever be in our hearts.

Chapter 11

$\mathcal{B}$EADELL FAMILY DESERT TRIPS

C OMMERCIAL desert safaris were not the only means by which Len was able to revisit the bush he cherished so dearly. Len and his family religiously undertook a pilgrimage to the far corner of an Australian desert almost every year from 1975 to 1993. Len's wife, Anne, and daughter, Connie, describe Len's philosophy towards the Beadell family desert trips and relate some of their experiences.

M OST of our trips were for a three-week period, usually encompassing the last week of the school term and the two-week school holiday period in May or August,' explains Anne. 'Len was prepared to sacrifice one week of the children's schooling because he felt they would learn more about life during a week in the bush than from the inevitable end-of-term wind-down. He viewed our camping trips as a real teaching experience for the children where they could learn how to be self-sufficient in the bush, how to camp and survive with limited resources, and how to conserve water.'

Connie continues: 'As children, we all loved the family desert trips. Gary in particular thought they were great because he didn't have to have a bath. Lenny was always very conservative with water; we were never allowed to wash ourselves unless either he could see we were all getting grumpy or he knew there was a water supply coming up soon. Occasionally we could wash our hair when we were one night away from civilisation. Jacqui, who was the youngest child, didn't enjoy the long spells of driving which we often endured early on in a desert trip; but once we stopped for the day she loved to collect firewood and help set up camp. Jacqui was a great finder of assorted objects including many of Lenny's spent cartridges from pistol flares, old tins from some of Lenny's original bush camp sites, and even a number of English coins from the former village at Emu. Camping represented a completely different lifestyle from that of everyday life. The food was different, there were vast open spaces, and we often didn't see another human being for up to two weeks. Lenny always planned our trips carefully to ensure that, over time, we saw every section of every road he built. He would delight in giving us a running commentary of where we were, as well as describing the history associated with each part of the desert. They were exciting family times together.'

However, there were certainly no home comforts on the Beadell family trips. Anne states: 'With up to five people in our Land Cruiser for three weeks at a time, there was simply not enough space for anything other than the bare essentials. We never took a fridge nor an esky. We ate fresh meat on the first day, but thereafter lived exclusively on tinned food. We took very few vegetables and never used margarine or butter. There was a strict allocation of 12 loaves of bread which were wrapped and made to last throughout the duration of the trip. A large tuckerbox, which Len made in 1957, took prime position in the back compartment of the vehicle. It was the first item that was unloaded each night. Inside there was a place for everything and everything remained in its place. The box contained jars for sugar, teabags, coffee, and jam, as well as powdered milk, washing up gear and cutlery. Len would simply take the box out of the car at the end of each trip and put it in his shed ready for the next expedition. Nothing was ever replaced between trips unless it ran out.

'Camping itself was primitive. We never took chairs on our family trips for many years. The children slept on the ground in a small scooped depression on our first trip, just as Len had done during his years in the bush. Len made a canvas awning to attach to the Toyota, but it provided no protection at all from the wind. He soon realised that he would have to provide the family with some better equipment if he wanted them to continue to come on his bush trips and so he attached a back flap to the awning, which worked very well. He carried numerous pieces of canvas of varying degrees of quality and waterproofing, one of which would be used as a ground sheet. We slept on the ground sheet in a line with our heads orientated to keep the wind off our faces. Initially we had a few blankets to keep ourselves warm in the invariably cold winter nights of late May and August. We later "splurged" on sleeping bags for the children, but never used swags. Len said they were simply too bulky and there wasn't enough room to carry them. This rudimentary method of camping remained standard practice for our family trips over nearly 20 years. Len argued that, if you were going into the desert country, then you had to experience the desert on its own terms. Luxuries of everyday life weren't part of the desert lifestyle.'

Connie continues: 'Lenny always carried our petrol in 12-gallon (60-litre) drums on the roof of the Land Cruiser. He never considered doing it any other way. He had no time for lots of little jerry cans or long-range fuel tanks. With drums, according to Lenny, we could alter the amount of fuel carried depending on where we were going. A long trip, for example, was always a "5-drum trip".'

As a general rule of thumb, we also never stopped more than one night in the same place. Lenny argued that, if there wasn't an engine to repair or a puncture to mend, then there was no reason not to move on. Mt Leisler in May 1976 however was a two-night stop. We decided to climb Mt Leisler as a family. Lenny had climbed the hill with Scotty (Boord) many years earlier and they had found a short-cut to the summit via a steep escarpment. Gary and I decided to attempt the short-cut, while Lenny, Anne and Jacqui (who was too young to climb) took the long route to the top. Gary and I reached the peak quickly and waited there for two hours for the others to arrive. All the while we had a clear view of our vehicle below. We were concerned that the rest of the family may have had an accident and so decided to go back to the vehicle via the long route. In the meantime, Lenny had similarly thought that Gary and I may have fallen or had an accident and he returned to the car with Anne and Jacqui before our arrival. A worried Lenny then headed back to climb Mt Leisler for a second time to look for us. We all eventually rendezvoused

Mark Shephard

The progress of this Beadell family trip was temporarily slowed by one of the local desert inhabitants.

Gary (far right) and his wife Ann-Indra, joined Connie, Len and Anne for a family trip to revisit the 250-mile centreline point in July 1993.

safely at the vehicle, but were exhausted from the day's adventure. Len was proud that we still had water left in our drink bottle at the end of the day. So Mt Leisler became a two-night stopover. A real treat!'

A special occasion for the family was the christening of Len's grandson Mitchell at Djindugara Rockhole in July 1992. Djindugara is situated in the heart of the Great Victoria Desert, 10 kilometres west of the South Australian/Western Australian border and a few hundred metres south of the Anne Beadell Highway. Len wrote a short account of the bush christening in the April/June 1993 issue of *Australian Geographic*. Part of this article is now reproduced.

S TANDING in the sandy red heart of the Great Victoria Desert, Father Alan Courtney stripped off his calico robe. He placed it on the camp table that served as a makeshift altar and then, wearing only shorts and a rough wooden cross hung around his neck with a leather bootlace, strode into the cold black waters of Djindugara Rockhole to perform one of Australia's most unusual baptisms.

I'd first visited Djindugara, a tiny oasis in a vast sea of sandhills and mulga some 600 kilometres west of Coober Pedy, South Australia, 30 years earlier when, with my wife, Anne and our five-month-old daughter, Connie Sue, I surveyed and supervised the building of the nearby 'highway' that I named after Anne.

When our youngest daughter, Jacqueline, and her husband, Russell Asser, had a son in January last year, they wanted to have young Mitchell baptised at a remote desert waterhole. Where better than Djindugara, beside the road named after his grandmother?

So last July, 16 friends and family members in five four-wheel-drive vehicles made the week-long journey to Djindugara. While we made camp, Janys Asser, Mitchell's other grandmother, made a cross of desert wildflowers that she glued to Father Courtney's plain white robe. I warmed a billy of Djindugara water to take the winter chill off it and poured it into a coolamon, the Aboriginal carrying dish we were using as a baptismal font.

Camel poison bush in the Great Victoria Desert.

Len drew this illustration to depict his search for the camel poison bush in the
Great Victoria Desert.

Carved from a bend in a bloodwood tree, it had been a treasured possession since I found it in the Great Sandy Desert in 1963.

Various members of the group read out appropriate Bible passages and then, accompanied by four recorders and a clarinet, we sang *The Lord Bless You* as Father Courtney trickled water over Mitchell's head. Neither the music nor the warm water allayed his hearty cries.

Later, as we shared a celebration lunch of apple damper and other treats, I hoped that one day Mitchell would derive just as much pleasure from telling his grandchildren about his special baptism as I had from participating in it. And that Djindugara would still be here, wild and unspoilt, for them to visit if they chose ...

O CCASIONALLY desert trips were arranged with a specific task or a particular theme in mind. In May 1989 Len and Anne, this time minus the children, ventured into the Great Victoria Desert to collect the leaves and bark of a tree named camel poison bush or wheelfruit *Gyrostemon ramulosus*. Camel poison bush is so named because its leaves are purported to be toxic to camels. The journals of early desert explorers, such as Ernest Giles, Lawrence Wells and David Lindsay for example, make reference to their camels becoming ill and dying after consuming leaves from this tree. However the exact nature of the leaf toxin has remained somewhat of a mystery. Dr Bryan Gatehouse, a chemist from Monash University, became interested in identifying the toxin after reading about the tree in one of Len's books, *Beating About The Bush*, page 145.

Bryan relates the story. 'I have long been interested in natural plant products and I wrote to Len to ask him if he could collect some leaves and bark from the camel poison bush if he ever came across a sufficient number of the bushes.

'In the interim I also wrote to the Northern Territory Herbarium in Alice Springs and they were able to send me enough leaves and stems to get started on an attempt to identify the toxic agent in the camel poison bush.

'An Honours chemistry student, Roger Misfud, undertook a

project to recover any natural products from the plant under the direction of Dr David Collins in our department. Eventually a small amount of material was obtained and a crystal was grown from the powder. I was able to determine by X-ray diffraction that the compound obtained was similar to codonocarpine. Whether this is the compound that kills camels is, of course, not yet known. We do not have many camels around here on which to test the compound!

'In the meantime Len had written to me to say that he had come across a stand of the trees in the Great Victoria Desert and offered to collect specimens for us. Three garbage bags of plant material duly arrived in the department together with a very unpleasant smell! I dried the material in a vacant area under a set of our lecture theatres and this nearly led to evacuation of the area, so bad was the smell.

'It is distinctly possible that the smell – similar to a sulphury mustard gas – was from the compound responsible for the death of the camels. If this were indeed the case then the very compound we were seeking may well have gone up into thin air during the drying process! Such is the way of science sometimes.

'A specimen from the material collected by Len was placed in the National Herbarium of Victoria (MEL). The specific MEL number is MEL 694274.'

Chapter 12

$\mathcal{F}$URTHER RECOLLECTIONS OF A GENTLE GIANT

L EN BEADELL touched the lives of countless thousands of Australians in so many ways. Everyone who met him, read his books or heard him speak took away a very special and personal memory of that experience. A cross-section of people who were fortunate to know Len at different times of his life, together with Len's family, have contributed their personal recollections of the giant of a man who, on the one hand, took on the Australian bush with a steely determination and toughness, yet at the same time remained gentle, compassionate and caring to all those around him.

John Whitehouse

John Whitehouse, a retired doctor who lived in the Blue Mountains in New South Wales for 42 years, knew Len perhaps longer than any other person. They were scouts together and their friendship remained through more than half a century.

M Y recollections of Len Beadell extend back to his teenage years, when he lived at 19 Eurella Street, Burwood. I first met Len after graduating from the wolf cubs to the Burwood Scouts, where Len was leader of the yellow robin patrol. All the Burwood patrols were named after birds at the time; and so there was a kookaburra patrol, the coachwhip patrol and the yellow robin patrol to name a few. Len was a great patrol leader; we called him the 'gink'. In those days, a 'gink' was a word used to describe someone who was a bit different. In Len's case, it wasn't used in a derogatory sense, but rather was a term of genuine affection for someone who really was different, yet so special. There only ever was and ever will be one Len Beadell!

We often had patrol competitions where a corner of the George
Street Scout Hall was set aside for each patrol to mount a display.
Len invariably decorated the 'yellow robin corner' with an array
of gadgets made at home using his forge and anvil and general
ironmongery skills; items such as miniature bridges, morse code
equipment, trail marking tools and iron knots. I recall how my
friends and I would religiously visit the Beadell home every

Len and John Whitehouse reunited at Len's 70th birthday party in 1993.

Saturday morning and marvel at Len's skill in being able to belt
the life out of a piece of red hot metal, trim bits off, and then
fashion it into another interesting object. Len's mother, who was
a very kind lady, always brought us orange drinks while we were
messing about in the backyard. Len's father was a quiet man of
small stature, with greying hair which was swept back neatly. I
remember Fred often rode his small Acme motor bike to the local
scout hall; I guess it was every boy's dream (including mine) to
own a motorbike in those days.

Len, myself and my friends soon came under the influence of a
very wonderful man by the name of John Theodore Chauncey

Richmond, sometimes known as JTCR, TC or JR. A bachelor, he was a short, thick-set man with a rounded, moon-shaped face and a crew cut. He worked as a surveyor for the Metropolitan Water Sewerage and Drainage Board of Sydney. Most importantly John Richmond was our scoutmaster and our idol as young boys. He taught us how to appreciate and understand the bush; he tutored us on bush skills including how to use a compass and read maps; he instilled in us a sense of self-sufficiency and self-reliance, and he fostered our love of camping. We took only the bare essentials to camp in those days, namely some blankets, a sweater for a pillow, a ground sheet and a small 'A' tent. Our parents simply couldn't afford to buy luxury items such as sleeping bags.

In addition to scouting camps, John Richmond regularly asked a privileged few to accompany him on weekend survey trips. Len was always there. He was like a son to John and a big brother to the rest of us. We'd head off in TC's little Morris wagon and later his 1936 Chevrolet Tourer. The survey trips were primarily to assist John's work with the Water Board, but they also enabled us to further hone our bush crafts under the guidance of a wonderful teacher.

The word *survey* became the integral part of Len's vocabulary in those days. For example, a haircut was a *survey* trim, a bicycle was a *survey* iron, and you'd take your *survey* coat on your *survey* trip in your *survey* wagon. The *survey* iron became a real status symbol in our group. Other boys had a mere bicycle, but we had a *survey* iron which was special because Mr Richmond and Lenny both said it was!

Len and his mentor,
John Richmond.

Len also described persons of the opposite gender as *fees*. According to Len, females or *fees* were *awkward* and he had nothing to do with *fees* because they only ever got you into trouble. The scouts often used to have game nights with the Burwood girl guides. They were great fun but Len would never attend because there were *fees* present.

Awkward was another term unique to Lenny's repertoire. He used it to describe something that was completely unacceptable to him. Len was a devout tea-totaller and so alcohol was *awkward*; wearing a hat to school was *awkward*, and, of course, there were those *fees*.

While mentioning the hat, Sydney Grammar had a strict policy of wearing a hat to and from school. Prefects manned the school gates to ensure the regulation was enforced. Len, of course, refused to wear his hat. He would carry it to school and pretend to scratch his head as he walked past the prefect each morning. (I might add that, after many decades of trying, I did eventually persuade Len to wear a hat in his later years in the desert).

Sadly the Second World War broke out in 1939. The army seconded our Scout Hall as a recruiting depôt and many of our scouting leaders, including Len, went to serve in the war. The influence of both the scouts and John Richmond's tutelage impacted permanently and profoundly on Len's philosophy and attitude towards life. He remained completely trustworthy. He would lend support to anyone who needed help. I never heard Len swear in the 50-plus years that I knew him. He showed humility when cast into the centre of attention. He always enjoyed a laugh. Finally, he liked nothing better than to sit around the campfire and tell stories; he held us spellbound with his campfire yarns when I was a lad and he was still captivating campfire audiences when I accompanied him on a Russell Guest tour some 50 years later.

Mind you, the first impressions that Len created with some people were not always favourable. Len would often call into my surgery in Springwood in the Blue Mountains during the Christmas holidays. Just as John Richmond had done many years earlier, Len would often bring a group of children with him. My secretary would undergo shock every time he appeared in his hob-nailed boots and khaki shorts, and there were always accompanying looks of amazement from patients in the waiting

Len continued to support the scout movement throughout his life, as evidenced by this poster he drew to promote a scout jamboree held at Woodhouse, near Adelaide, in October 1987.

room. Everything was put on hold until I had a chance to catch up with Len and his youthful contingent.

Soon after I was married and, while I was still completing my medical degree, my wife and I lived in a small flat in Croydon near Sydney. There was a knock at the front door one day. My wife opened the door. A cackling giant of a man, dressed in huge boots and great khaki shorts, greeted her. She had never met Len before. She said to me: 'Oh, my God, are all you're friends like this?' I replied 'It's all right. It's only the gink!'

Leon Hoare

Leon Hoare initially met Len while working as a Medical Officer at Woomera in 1952. He remained a long-term friend of Len and his family. Leon provides an insight into life in the early days of the Outback township and reflects on Len's character.

IN 1952, three years after graduating from the Adelaide Medical School, I took up employment as Medical Officer at Woomera, working under the then Senior Medical Officer, Colonel Bloomfield. At this time, Woomera was a small town with well-built houses and paved streets lined with native saplings which were watered daily by a water truck. Service personnel included elements of the Australian Army, Navy and Air Force, and there were attachments of personnel from the British and United States Armed Services as well as scientists from all three countries involved in rocketry.

There was a large contingent of workers employed by the Department of Works who were engaged in road construction and other building activities. The general population of Woomera also included wives and children of both Service personnel and civilians, as well as others involved in running the Officer's Mess, the Sergeant's Mess and the Ordinary Ranks Mess. It was essentially a place of relatively young people with quite a high birth rate. There were Padres representing most religions and I particularly remember Howell Witt who, even then, was known as 'The Bish.'

The Service Messes were corrugated iron buildings equipped with Bonaire evaporative air conditioners which were quite suitable in the dry climate. The Messes were conducted with full Service tradition and the food was good. There was no shortage of alcohol.

In my capacity as Medical Officer, I was paid a salary of about £1 900 a year to look after all the Service personnel. Colonel Bloomfield left Woomera for personal reasons in about July or August 1952. I remained as the Senior Medical Officer, and was soon joined by Dr Dion Manthorpe for the remainder of the year, which provided just as happy an arrangement as I had experienced with Colonel Bloomfield.

Off duty, there were many things to do. There were trips to the station country to visit places like Roxby Downs, where meat was available to be brought into the Mess; to Koolymilka, and to Arcoona Station, where the Moody's had a wonderful opal collection.

Out of that country one day came a tall, gangly, cackling, shaven-headed individual with a laugh and personality to be remembered – Lenny Beadell. Wearing an open-necked khaki shirt, shorts and boots without socks, he would stride about with a cheery word and a smile and a laugh which was quite infectious.

On Saturday evenings there would be the cinema to attend; instead of rushing out to buy sweets during interval, many children would remain around Lenny as he told them funny stories and handed them sweets which he would keep in his pocket just for them. It was as though Father Christmas had come to Woomera every Saturday night; the children's eyes would light up, they would call out to Lenny, and crowd around him as though he was the Pied Piper.

Len and I became great friends. He would always come to me to have his medical equipment checked out before travelling off for weeks at a time into the untrammelled Outback, where he would undertake astrosurveys in setting out the perimeters of the Woomera Rocket Range.

The Messes were conducted with due decorum and, after 5pm,

it was mandatory to wear neat summer attire with shoes and socks. Lenny bent to this requirement by carrying in his pocket a pair of sock tops, which had the foot section of the sock removed. He used to pull these over his boots and tuck the sock top into his boots, so as to give the appearance of wearing a normal sock. He simply liked to feel the leather of his boots around his feet. The trick provided considerable amusement for overseas visitors.

During my time at Woomera it was very apparent that the humble exterior of Lenny Beadell hid a thoughtful, caring and highly respected person with unique skills as a surveyor. And his skills were well recognised, particularly by the authorities and scientists from Great Britain, with whom he mingled freely and who later invited him to return to Great Britain where he was fêted beyond his usual station.

Len learnt surveying from colleagues whilst in the army in New Guinea; and he never ceased telling me of his admiration for these tutors. Len was particularly devoted to his parents. During his holidays from Woomera he would drive down to Adelaide, pick up his father from Salisbury and then take him on something of a bushman's picnic, right into the Outback again where both of them would enjoy the silent areas in which Lenny himself worked all year.

Len's private car at the time was a post-war model Chevrolet. He eventually decided to upgrade this vehicle and came to Adelaide with a view to purchasing a Chrysler Royal which, in the fashion of the time, had large fins on each rear mudguard. He visited the sales room where they also sold small British standard sedans. His approach to the salesman in his usual khaki shorts, shirt and boots without socks led the salesman to direct him repeatedly to the small standard cars and away from the Chrysler Royals. But Lenny's insistence finally prevailed and he was allowed to look over a Chrysler Royal. And, with a cackle, he said: 'I'll take one of those.'

The salesman asked him to provide some detail of his credit, whereupon he reached into his hip pocket, pulled out a bunch of one hundred pound notes and proceeded to peel them off, much to the absolute surprise of the salesman. He halted before paying the final hundred pound note. He looked the salesman in the eye and, again with a cackle, said the only proviso in completing the sale would be that the salesman must arrange to weld a reinforcing rod between the two fins at the back of the Chrysler on which he could hang his water bags. With some protestation and injured pride, the salesman was forced to accede to Lenny's request, and he was paid the final one hundred pound note.

Lenny and I both had many humorous and enlightening conversations with Padre Howell Witt who, being Welsh, spoke with the undulating lilt of that accent and could embellish and tell a story with every skill of the acting stage.

Michael Breen, the civilian Mayor of Woomera in those days, was himself a character. He taught me how to play shove-halfpenny. This was a dangerous game because it was played for a round of liqueurs and often went on until the early hours of the morning. He would also walk to the showers in the morning like the rest of us in the single men's quarters, but would resist removing his toupée until hidden within the confines of the shower closet.

One previous Medical Officer had been thought to be diabetic because of the frequency with which he would return to his hut in order to drink from his water bag. It was soon noted that he would develop something of a staggering gait after these frequent visits. Finally, some curious chap had a taste of the fluid in the water bag and discovered it contained a high percentage of gin.

Two characters, George Neal and Bunny Hodge of the Royal Australian Navy, remain in my mind because of their ebullient personalities. I would often visit Eunice and George Neal in their home for a meal which was somewhat more extravagant than could be provided by the Mess. I was regularly accompanied by Tony Morris who was the President of the Officer's Mess at that time. He was a balding Englishman with a ruddy smile and ever-present wit who, towards the end of the roast beef, relished dipping his bread in the bleeding juice of the carving dish to such an extent that it was worth travelling miles to see.

Lenny Beadell was well-known and loved by all these

characters, and indeed by everyone with whom he came in contact at Woomera. His cheerful personality was so uplifting to all those whom he met. His penetrating and caring insight will always be remembered by myself, my colleagues at Woomera, and those who had the good fortune to encounter him as a friend.

Christmas cards from Woomera, drawn by Len.

Reverend Howell Witt

Howell Witt was the Anglican Minister at Woomera for many years and a true character in his own right. He continues the Woomera story. Len and Howell developed a special friendship, which later saw Howell act as celebrant at Len's wedding.

I first met Len at a dinner in the Officers Mess at Woomera. I was a newcomer to the town and was soon made aware that 'dining in' at the Mess was somewhat of an event. I noticed that one gentleman at the dinner appeared different to everyone else, as he was wearing civilian garb. I felt for him and so I decided to take him under my wing. I later realised how silly I was. I'd only been in the town for a month and here I was, as I soon found out, advising the man who'd discovered and surveyed the place. Maybe it was then that Len took me under his wing!

For some years I ran the local scout group at Woomera. Len was always there, explaining maps and other mysteries of the stars and the bush to the youths. We often took the boys to the local picture theatre. Len loved Abbott and Costello. He also had a loud laugh. A deaf man would have known Beadell was at the flicks and comedy was on the cards. Pimba probably knew too!

But that picture theatre brought Len and me closer. Woomera officers were once summoned there for a lecture to be given, not by one of a higher rank, but by a public servant. Intellectual? Maybe. Incomprehensible? You can say that again! A fellow officer approached me after the lecture and said: 'Well, that clears it up.'

'Not for me' I replied.

'You heard him,' stated the officer.

'Heard, yes; understood, no!' I said.

'They're going to let off an atomic bomb up in the scrub at X200 [the future site of Emu],' replied the officer.

So I asked Len where X200 was and how one got there. Len stated: 'Would you like to visit the area? I'll drive.' I still don't know where we went, but it was the drive of a lifetime. And then there was the haircut. My father once said to me that my hair would disappear before I was much older. His prophecy was fulfilled half way between Woomera and X200 when Len decided to cut my hair!

Len had been sent to Woomera at the end of the war along with a number of other returned soldiers awaiting discharge. They were told their discharge papers would be sent to the nearest post office. Weekly they drove to that post office, some 50 miles away. And one day the papers did arrive. The soldiers greeted their arrival joyfully. Envelopes were ripped open frantically and there were shouts of glee. Free at last and back to the big smoke. Only one soldier didn't join in the celebrations. He never opened his envelope, but respectfully handed it back to the lady at the post office. He'd been surveying in the bush all his life and he wanted to continue doing so. The big smoke was no place for Len Beadell.

My friendship with Len continued to blossom over the years and I was fortunate to be asked to marry Len and his wife Anne. What could possibly go wrong at a wedding, I thought? So there we were: one bride, one groom, a best man, a bevy of bridesmaids and myself as celebrant. I said to the groom: 'Take her by the right hand.' So he took her by the left. 'Try again,' I said. 'With your right hand take Anne's right hand.' With his left hand he took her right! 'Let's try one more time,' I pleaded. 'With your right hand ... your RIGHT hand ...' His left hand came forward again. I was sure it was the bride's beauty that was confusing him. 'With the NORTH one,' I said. And he did it, just like that!'

David Hewitt

David Hewitt worked with Aboriginal communities in South Australia, the Northern Territory and Western Australia from the 1960s to 1986. He is a keen historian and is well-known in Outback circles for his interest in the Canning Stock Route. In 1983 David and a team of enthusiasts completely restored Well 26 on the famous trail. He later contributed to Australian Geographic's *book on the Stock Route.*

I FIRST met Len Beadell in 1964, while I was working at the South Australian Government Aboriginal settlement of Musgrave Park (now Amata in the Anangu Pitjantjatjara Lands). Only months earlier Len had completed the last of his network of Outback roads, far to the north-west of the Musgrave Ranges.

It was an era before four-wheel-drive tourists and I quickly developed a real respect for the remoteness of the Outback and the people who travelled there. I took every opportunity to find out all I could about the country from people who passed through Amata. The name of Len Beadell was constantly mentioned and I became keen to meet the man, whom I felt was a bit of a legend. Staff from the Giles Meteorological Station told me about his murals on their Mess room walls. Survey teams from the Division of National Mapping, who regularly filled with fuel and water at Amata, always talked about his roads. Walter MacDougall, a Native Patrol Officer at Woomera, spoke about an adventurous early reconnaissance with him, while Aboriginal men from Warburton, with whom I was working, knew Len well and admired his achievements. Our settlement at Amata had been built three years earlier near the eastern end of Len's best-known road, the Gunbarrel Highway.

So it was a pleasant surprise to meet the man responsible for all this in my first year in the area.

In 1965 Len acted as a guide for the well-known anthropologist, Donald Thomson, on an expedition to the Gibson Desert. The party passed through Amata on their way south at the conclusion of this trek. Stepping out of a Land Rover with Commonwealth number plates was a fellow in an old pair of shorts and boots, but no socks!

Len was not well but, in a way which I found out later was typical of the man, he made light of an illness that was to keep him out of the bush for the next few years. The small staff at Amata were always pleased to see visitors and Len was the life of the party over a cup of tea with Donald Thomson's group.

The following year the message reached the Western Deserts that Len's first book, *Too Long in the Bush*, was about to be published. Just before Christmas 1965, I was passing through

An example of Len's artwork in the Giles mess room.

Adelaide on holidays and enquired at the John Martins book department about *Too Long in the Bush*. The sales assistant handed over a copy of the book and said: 'Don't tell me you know this fellow too.' The book had only been available for a few months, but there had been a constant stream of people through John Martins who knew Len Beadell, related stories about him to the staff, or were keen to get hold of a copy of his first book. His reputation had spread far and wide even in those early days.

Soon after, while on a study tour to Malaysia, I ran into a British Army officer who had met Len during the bomb tests at Maralinga. I mentioned the book to him. If it was going to be 'embellished with Len's cartoons' he definitely had to have it. On returning to Australia, I sent him a copy which became one of his prized possessions.

We were fortunate to know some of the men who worked with Len through the road building years. They included Frank Quinn, or just simply Quinny, the supply driver and owner of Lassie the dog, who herself was acknowledged on some of Len's aluminium plaques. In later years Frank had the contract to cart fuel from Alice Springs to Giles. He was a remarkable bush mechanic and a character in his own right. Over many cups of tea at Amata and later Docker River, he was able to enlarge on stories which, no doubt because of publishing constraints, received only brief mention in Len's books.

Five years later we were working at Docker River, to the west of Ayers Rock, when Len started guiding visitors on his roads with Adelaide-based tour operators, Dick Lang and Rex Ellis. Len was always interested in what was happening along the roads and took every opportunity to gather information from people living and working in the area. Usually portrayed as a great talker, he was also a keen listener.

Len once said that he always tried to place his road junctions at scenic locations. One such junction that we always enjoyed, and passed almost weekly during our four years at Docker, was the start of the Sandy Blight Junction Road, south of Giles. One of Len's trademark signposts, painted white, stands among a beautiful grove of desert oaks with the dark hue of the Rawlinson Range in the background.

If Len's roads happened to run close to a mature bloodwood or desert oak, then these trees were usually the recipient of a plaque. In the days when desert travellers were few and far between, these signs gave a sense of reassurance to people travelling his roads for the first time, confirming that they really were where they hoped to be!

In later years on infrequent visits to Adelaide, we looked forward to catching up with Len, sometimes at an evening at Dick Lang's home at Highbury. They were times of long discussions late into the night and always full of laughter, with Len often holding the floor.

My wife, daughter and I last saw Len at Well 33 on the Canning Stock Route in July 1994. We were heading in one direction and Len in the other. He was leading yet another group of four-wheel-drive enthusiasts along some of his roads – and keeping up a cracking pace. This was to be one of Len's last trips to his beloved bush. Connie was with him and, since Len's death, a number of his supporters have no doubt been delighted to see her carrying on the family tradition.

Throughout his working life Len followed the example of the words in one of his favourite hymns:

> Guide me O thou great redeemer,
> Pilgrim through this barren land.

At Len's funeral service I was fortunate to sit next to a man (Kevin) who had known Len from the early days of Woomera. I had to catch a plane soon after the service. Kevin offered to drive me a considerable distance to Adelaide airport and much out of his way. I would have missed the last flight for the day to Canberra without his help. As someone whom he had met for the first time just a little over an hour earlier, I was very grateful indeed. Kevin refused to take payment for his trouble, saying: 'Len would have done the same.'

Such was Len's leadership.

Peter Wenham

Peter Wenham, an architectural designer from Adelaide, has been a devout fan of Len's since his childhood. In 1988 Peter was a participant in a safari organised by Dick Lang to commemorate the 30th Anniversary of the building of the Gunbarrel Highway. Len and Anne Beadell were guests of that tour.

I T was one of those nights that country people take for granted but, for those of us who only visit the bush, we remember for the rest of our lives. The heat of the day was long gone, and there was a dampness in the air which settled on everything beyond the direct glow of the campfire. I turned my back to the fire and looked towards the heavens to appreciate the glory of the clear moonless sky. Some of the other campers had already drifted off to their tents and, in the first lull in conversation since dawn, I asked Len if it was possible to tell the time by the Southern Cross.

I had known about Len Beadell for more than 25 years, though we had only met in the last few days.

As a boy, I had attended a Christian Men's Fellowship slide-evening at which Len was the guest speaker. Enthralled by his enthusiasm for his topic, his sense of humour, and his absolute love of the bush, I was hooked. Immediately afterwards I read those of Len's books which were available, and was amazed to learn of his ability to establish his exact position, anywhere on the face of the earth, merely by looking at the stars.

Years later, still intrigued by the mysteries of positional astronomy, I purchased an old theodolite at a government auction, and set about finding out exactly where I was. My wife and children will attest to the many holiday camp nights I spent in the cold with the theodolite's night illuminators plugged into the battery of the Land Rover, the one-second beeps from the short-wave radio time signals piercing the bush silence, and the spirit of Len Beadell to spur me on. I never did get the same result twice! Whilst the task no longer holds secrets for me, the wonder of it has never left.

When the opportunity to go on an Outback safari trip along the famed Gunbarrel Highway arose, I didn't take too much persuading. The occasion was the 30th anniversary of the surveying of that area of Outback Australia, with no less than Len Beadell himself as guest traveller. I had never thought that now, after so many years, I would finally get to meet my hero. One of the most memorable times of my life was spent with a mixed group of twenty or so people, all of whom I remember, can still name, and are happy to call friends. Once a year, for years afterwards, we gathered with our families for a weekend or a barbecue or such, to relive the experience of that trip. I realised then the consummate ability of Len to attract, mix with, and get along with people from all walks of life. It didn't matter if it was an old friend, or someone he had just met, Len would put them at ease, and talk to them as a friend. I noticed particularly his ability to talk to my children, quietly on their own, and show a genuine interest in them as individuals, and about what they were doing.

Mark Shephard

Len, keenly watched by Anne and Dick Lang, cuts the celebratory cake to commemorate the 30th anniversary of the completion of the Gunbarrel Highway, Mungilli Claypan, Gibson Desert, May 1988.

And so it was that Len jumped up from his spot by the campfire and, with his inimitable enthusiasm for a subject so dear to his heart, started on a long treatise about time, first points of Aries, days since some epoch or other, and angles (estimated only) between the major axis of the Southern Cross and some imaginary plumb line. The saga went on and on, with various anecdotes thrown in, but always returning to the topic in hand. After 25 minutes or so, he finally reached the conclusion, taking into account all of the factors he had been discussing (and, I suspect, some he hadn't) that, by his calculations, he estimated the present time to be ... 10:32 pm.

In was in fact only 10:30 pm. I have never found out whether he misjudged the angles of the stars, miscalculated the time that it would take to complete telling the story, or simply couldn't read anyone's watch in the dark.

That was the Len Beadell I had known and admired for so long, and was now privileged to call a friend.

Marie Mahood

Marie Mahood, and her husband Joe, first met Len Beadell in 1956. Joe was a stock inspector at both Finke and Alice Springs. Len befriended the Mahoods and regularly stayed with them during visits to the Centre. Marie herself is an author of renown, having written seven books with outback themes. She now lives at Cattle Camp Station, inland from Mackay, Queensland.

IN all the years my husband and I knew Lenny, we only ever saw him in his standard garb of short-sleeved shirt, shorts, boots and sock tops over the boots. His voice and frequent laugh were pitched for the open spaces.

Lenny was the nearest equivalent to the Pied Paper I have ever known. He would park his vehicle in our yard at Finke and then later at Alice Springs, and within half an hour children would appear as if drawn by a magnet. Our own children were no exception.

Lenny was a complete individual but he had a gift, a very rare gift, of being able to instantly talk at any level with anyone, including children, Aboriginal people or adults from any and every walk of life. He was so genuinely interested in everything around him, especially the bush, and its people; and he had a warmth that drew an instant response.

He also had the slightly twisted sense of humour and the ability to handle the unexpected situations which crop up regularly in the bush and would defeat the ordinary man.

We knew Lenny in the 1950s before his marriage and considered him among our closest friends.

Len made our home a base on his infrequent visits to Alice Springs and he entertained us with many anecdotes of his bush trips, visits to 'the city' and later his trip around the world, where he stayed in England with Lord and Lady Penney. He said Lady Penney pestered him, just like I did, with offers to wash his shirt. (I think he only had two, the one he wore and the one in his swag). Lenny was what, in the old days, we used to call one of Nature's Gentlemen.

And a final brief tribute to the Gentle Giant of the bush from Len's children, Connie, Gary and Jacqui.

Connie Beadell

L EN was a wondrous father, unique in many ways. I don't remember ever calling him anything but Lenny – that's what kids always called him! My friends didn't have a father who wrote books, gave talks to thousands of people a year, drew huge cards for their birthdays, didn't swear, drink or smoke, or take them on desert trips for their school holidays. They especially didn't have roads named after them.

As a teenager, when Len (complete with cheeky grin) introduced me to people as 'the baby in the bucket' (referring to my photo in his book *Bush Bashers*), I felt a keen sense of embarrassment. It's something I had to work hard at overcoming! He had a quirky sense of humour that kept us forever laughing, as well as the courage of his convictions regardless of what other people might say. It was these things, together with his love of freedom and independence, and absolute confidence in his abilities as a surveyor, that kept him going year after year through the difficult conditions he faced in the desert. Now, as I get further into my research of Len's work on a day-to-day basis through his diaries, I feel a renewed sense of respect and intense pride in his achievements, and feel privileged to be the 'baby in the bucket!'

Throughout his life, another trait he had was to help others. He was always helping people plan desert trips, or mending anything from toys to false teeth to cuckoo clocks. Nothing was thrown away at home until he had either had a go at mending it first or he was sure it wouldn't be useful someday – a true bushman's trait. He would also make things himself if at all possible – they were always much stronger than items purchased from a shop!

My memories of our early desert trips are precious for the very reasons explained in the previous chapter. We learned the value of life, nature and family in a way that could never have been taught at school, and we learnt them well. Those trips were also a glimpse into Len's past. Considering the lack of bathing on those trips, I was lucky to have even got that bath in the bucket all those years ago! As he used to say: 'You make the roads, then you take your family on them for holidays!'

Gary Beadell

I T was always good to be able to tell friends at school that we were going bush for the school holidays. They usually had that slightly quizzical look on their faces, as they didn't comprehend what we were doing; going to a great expanse of nothing to do, well, 'what?' In our teenage years, the idea of going on holiday with 'The Olds' also seemed strange – you weren't suppose to do that sort of thing then. I know my friends were envious, more because we were doing something out of the ordinary than the actual experience itself.

Bush trips were always a great time for the family as a unit. To be together even for a few weeks a year in our increasingly busy lives, devoid of TV, radio, sports and other social distractions, was immensely valuable and continues our good relations to this day, and indeed, for the future.

Lenny was outstanding in his way of teaching two-way respect. If you respected and looked after your vehicle, it would look after you. If you loved and respected the bush folk; the station people, Aboriginal people, Giles' scientists or whoever; you would engender great loyalty and warmth in return. You only had to see how people brightened up and greeted our vehicle when they saw Lenny at the wheel to appreciate this. If you loved and respected nature and the environment it would open its treasures for you to marvel at. These aspects we could carry back to our day-to-day lives at home.

Jacqui Asser

I N growing up with Lenny as my father, I was always immensely proud of the exciting things that Lenny achieved. I also admired him for the person he was and I always tried to be more like him.

Both of my parents are very special people and Connie, Gary and I were fortunate enough to grow up in a close loving family.

If you knew Lenny at all, you would understand that he lived by some simple basic values. These values became a part of our family lives and were integral to our upbringing. Some of these include: being honest and sincere in all things you do and with all people you meet; acknowledging that all people are special and should be treated with kindness and friendliness; and always offering to lend a helping hand to anyone you are capable of helping. As you can imagine, having a sense of humour was very important; it not only makes you feel better yourself but makes everyone around you feel good as well. Also, don't waste anything [from left-over food to spare nuts and bolts] and certainly never throw anything out unless it really can't be fixed. Finally, don't waste the talents you have been given and the skills you have learned; and believe in yourself always. You never fail unless you haven't tried.

As a parent myself, I look back on these values and have tried to make them a part of my own children's lives, just as they were an important part of mine. I encourage Mitchell and Courtney to grow up into people I know my parents would be proud of. Lenny delighted in teaching us things – from lighting a fire to pointing out various star constellations – and he would always make time to spend with us. This perhaps is the most important value of all and we knew he loved us as much as we all loved him. I know his love and his teachings will stay with us and our children always.

Chapter 13

MILESTONES

T HERE are many other memorable events or 'milestones' which occurred throughout the last 40 years of Len's life. A number of these milestones are now listed in chronological order and with brief support information. Some emphasise Len's personal achievements, some reflect more on his character, while others relate to family events which were so important to Len.

13 April 1959: British Empire Medal

Len's achievements in surveying and opening up the Australian Outback were formally recognised when he was announced as a

recipient of the British Empire Medal in the Queen's Birthday Honours List in June 1958. He received the Medal on 13 April 1959 from Sir William Slim at a ceremony held at Government House in Adelaide. Len's father attended the presentation.

Len proudly wearing his British Empire Medal.

1 September 1971: Len first met his sporting idol, Sir Donald Bradman

Len presented a lecture to the Adelaide Rotary Club in September 1971. The lecture was attended by Sir Donald and Lady Bradman, who were members of the club. Sir Donald was one of Len's sporting idols and, like many Australians of that era, Len had spent many nights listening attentively to English radio broadcasts of Ashes battles against the Old Dart. More than a decade and a half later, on 23 March 1988, Len was guest speaker at the annual Bradman Medal Dinner, where Sir Donald presented the medal named in his honour to Paul Nobes as the South Australian District Cricketer of the Year. Sir Donald signed several books for Len's son Gary after the dinner.

22 July 1973: Lecture at Government House, Adelaide

Len was invited by Sir Mark and Lady Oliphant to present a lecture at Government House, Adelaide, in July 1973. Len had previously talked to the Girl Guides Association of South Australia, of which Lady Oliphant was Patron. The usual black-tie formality of a Government function was dispensed with on that July night, partly to accommodate Len who at the time didn't own a dinner suit. Sir Mark struck an immediate rapport with Len. He later wrote the Foreword to one of Len's books *Still In The Bush* and prepared a letter of recommendation for Len's Order of Australia Award nomination (see later).

Len with the family's first four-wheel-drive, a Toyota Land Cruiser LC.

31 May 1975: The Beadell's First Four-Whcel-Drive Vehicle Arrives

Len drove Land Rovers exclusively during his survey work in the Australian deserts. During a visit to Leigh Creek in 1974, Len first saw the Toyota Land Cruiser. He was immediately impressed by its large overall size and solid build. The Beadell's first Toyota, a Land Cruiser LC, was ordered on 27 July 1974 [at a cost of $6 300] and collected on 31 May 1975. Three months later, the family headed north for their inaugural family desert trip.

15 March 1979: A Second Family Four-Wheel-Drive

A new Toyota Land Cruiser FJ55 was purchased in March 1979. It served the Beadell's well over the ensuing two decades, clocking up over 185 000 kilometres of desert travel during that time. The vehicle remains with the Beadell family today.

22 November 1984: Royal Commission into British Nuclear Tests in Australia

Len was required to present evidence to the 1984 royal commission into the British Nuclear testing programme in Australia during the late 1950s - early 1960s. He spent four hours in the dock, where he was instructed by his legal representative 'to liven up the proceedings.' Len was asked to talk specifically about his work in laying out fence lines and surveying a network of boundary roads in the restricted areas around Maralinga. These roads were regularly patrolled by security officers to ensure that Service or civilian personnel did not enter such areas. During the years following the royal commission, Len refused to take sides on the issue of whether radiation exposure had been responsible for subsequent health problems experienced by Service personnel. However he believed that the scientists did know what they were doing, and that personnel were encouraged to take precautions.

1 June 1985: Bourke to Burketown Bash

Len flew to Sydney to officially start the Bourke to Burketown Bash. He was the Guest of Honour on the Bash.

29 June 1986: 25th Wedding Anniversary

Len's children, Jacqui and Gary, organised a surprise party for their parent's 25th Wedding Anniversary. (Connie was overseas at the time). Gary took Len and Anne to their regular Sunday morning church service while Jacqui set up for the party at home. Even though Gary drove home via a friend's house and entered their Salisbury home via the back door, Len and Anne never smelt a rat! Len was greatly surprised to be greeted by numerous old friends and family members; and he cherished the memory of that occasion.

6 January 1987: Daughter Jacqui's first teaching appointment

Len's daughter Jacqui took up her first teaching appointment at the Woomera Area School (where else?) in early 1987. An article featuring Len and Jacqui soon appeared in the 9 February edition of *Gibber Gabber*, the local magazine to which Len had contributed so much during Woomera's formative years.

Jacqui recalls: 'After completing my final year of Teacher's College, I was prepared to go anywhere in the state to take up my first teaching post. I never imagined that I would be asked to go to the Woomera Area School! The man who notified me of my appointment by phone tried to tell me a little of the history of Woomera. I told him I knew all about it, but I don't think he ever believed me! I was thrilled and Lenny, of course, was very excited and proud. I was very disappointed to be moved to Whyalla the following year, because it had been a truly wondrous year. We used to say tongue-in-cheek that Lenny built the township of Woomera so that I could have somewhere to begin my teaching career!'

20 November 1987: Honorary Fellow of the Institute of Engineering and Mining Surveyors (FIEMS)

Len was awarded Honorary Fellowship of the Institute of Engineering and Mining Surveyors (IEMS) Australia Inc, following the National Council Meeting on 20 October 1987. He formally received his Membership Certificate at the Annual General Meeting of the South Australian Division of the IEMS one month later, on 20 November. It was the South Australian Division who had recommended to the National Council that Len be admitted as an Honorary Fellow. Len regarded this award very highly as it indicated to him that his contribution to the field of surveying had been recognised by his peers.

20 April 1988: Retirement from Defence Science and Technology Organisation (DSTO)

Len was determined not to retire from work until the last day before his 65th birthday. Around 100 people, including many

Len receives a caricature of himself from Don Bennier, on his retirement from the DSTO, April 1988.

former retirees, attended his farewell barbecue lunch at the Salisbury office of the DSTO on 20 April 1988. Len was presented with an Omega watch, a full set of aeronautical (1:1 000 000) maps of Australia, his beloved Tavistock theodolite and tripod, and other gifts. Several of the carpenters in the workshop also made a coffee table for Len, which was given to him earlier that week. The following extracts are taken from letters written to Len on his retirement:

Len drew this illustration to accompany the notice advertising the function organised for his retirement.

From Bob Ramsay, Director of the Surveillance Research Laboratory of DSTO's Salisbury office:

Your preliminary survey work, performed in trying conditions during 1947-48 and from 1950 up to the mid sixties, and your contributions to the establishment of Woomera, various test sites such as Maralinga, and inland roads, are widely known. This work performed by you so ably with enormous dedication was also much valued, as indicated by the expressions of appreciation conveyed to you from the then Chief Scientist, the Secretary and the Minister of Supply through the Controller LRWE in 1955.

DSTO, and in particular the Illustrations Section, where you spent some twenty years of your later working life, will no doubt miss your friendly presence, vast knowledge of the Outback, artistic capabilities and seeing that little lizard on all the posters around the area! You will be remembered as being an integral part of the history of Woomera and this establishment, as well as for your literary and other achievements.

From Henry d'Assumpacao, Office of the Chief Scientist at DSTO's Canberra Head Office

For so long you have been an integral part of the DSTO, in particular DSTO Salisbury. Your contributions began in the very earliest days of LWRE and have continued up to the present. The Gunbarrel Highway will stand as a permanent reminder of your achievements.

Your second career in the drafting area is also distinguished, but for different reasons. For decades the hallmark of success has been to own a Lenny Beadell cartoon. (I pride myself that I actually have two)!

Apart from your talents and your achievements, I can say confidently that everybody has enjoyed your humour and enthusiasm and I hope that retirement won't slow you down or deter you from continuing your lecturing and the writing of books.

I consider myself honoured to have been associated with you and find it hard to imagine DSTO without you.

May - July 1988: A Double Dose of Wedding Bells

Two of Len's children, Gary and Jacqui, were married during a three-month period in mid 1988. Len drew special invitations for both weddings.

Gary and Ann-Indra Anthony were married at St Pius X Catholic Church, Dernancourt, Adelaide, on 15 May 1988. The Beadell's Toyota FJ55 was the official bridal car. Ann, who was small in frame, needed a box to climb in and out of the vehicle on the day. The Beadell's had only just returned from a desert trip. Len was not one for regularly cleaning his vehicle, and two days of solid cleaning were required to remove nine years of ingrained red bulldust to prepare the vehicle for the occasion. On the morning of the wedding, ribbons were tied from the roof rack to the bull bar. White flowers were placed in a temporary vase, made from waterpipe and fastened to the bullbar by a vice. Len drove Ann

Len drew this illustration for Gary's wedding invitation.

to the church. Gary played the organ with Connie while waiting for his bride to arrive, while Connie played the first movement from Bach's E major violin concerto [one of Len's favourites] during Ann's entrance to the church. Father Norbert Olson performed the marriage ceremony. Sometime later, Father Olson ran into Len again at Ayers Rock and greeted him like an old friend. Len didn't recognise him, partly because he was wearing civvies [desert gear] at the time. Len asked: 'Now where do I always see you?' To which Father Olson replied: 'Well, I married your son!'

Around 140 people attended Gary and Ann's wedding reception, which also represented a farewell party to the newly-weds as they were leaving for Germany two days later. They initially intended to stay in Germany for 18 months but remained overseas for nine and a half years, returning to Adelaide just before Christmas 1997.

Len's daughter Jacqui married Russell Asser on 3 July 1988 in a more formal ceremony at St Barbara's Anglican Church, Parafield Gardens, Adelaide. Jacqui endured a trying time leading up to the

Gary and Ann-Indra on their wedding day. The Beadell family Toyota, resplendent with ribbons and flowers, was the formal bridal car for the occasion.

wedding. Len was initially determined to wear his desert boots for the occasion, while Jacqui insisted that he should wear a pair of 'shiny black pointy shoes' which he loathed. [The last time Len wore them was at his own wedding]! Right up until two weeks before the wedding, Len let Jacqui think he was going to give her away in those desert boots. She pleaded and begged with him, but he remained outwardly obstinate. Of course he had every intention of changing his shoes. In the end he went to the local shoe store and bought a pair of black shoes which were 'less pointy!'

Jacqui states: 'There was a great excitement and an air of anticipation in the Church of St Barbara's just before I walked down the aisle holding nervously onto Lenny's arm.

'Our guests were more interested to know what Len was wearing than what my dress was like! But the biggest thrill for me was to see him in polished black leather shoes!'

15 September 1988: Ceremony at the 'Centre of Gravity' of Australia

Len was an invited guest of the Royal Geographical Society of Queensland at a ceremony held on Lilla Creek Station, west of Finke in the Northern Territory, to unveil a flag pole and plaque marking the 'geographic centre' or 'centre of gravity' of Australia.

Adelaide historian Bruce Macdonald provides the following background information on the project:

The Geographic Centre of Australia was established in 1988 as a bi-centennial project of the Royal Geographical Society of Queensland.

The 'Geographic Centre' is best described as the planometric centre of gravity of mainland Australia. In other words, if one was to paste a map of Australia onto a card, cut out the outline and then find the point at which the map balances, then this is the planometric centre of gravity.

The actual calculation of the centre point was based on the identification by co-ordinates of approximately 24 000 points along the Australian coastline and then computing the data to determine the point which divided equally the longitudinal and latitudinal halves of the country. A suitable mathematical formula was derived and the mathematical process was carried out by computing staff of the Queensland Department of Mapping and Surveying at the request of the Queensland Society. The computation took many months of computer analysis.

Having obtained the co-ordinates of the centre point, the Northern Territory Department of Mapping and Surveying provided the field crew and resources to physically locate the point on the ground. The location of the centre point is:

Latitude 25° 36' 36.4" S
Longitude 134° 21' 17.3" E

A commemorative flag pole, based on the design of the flag pole on Parliament House in Canberra, was erected on the site on Lilla Creek Station near the Finke to Kulgera Travelling Stock Route about 45 kilometres west of Finke. The centre point was named the Lambert Centre in recognition of the services to mapping by Bruce Lambert, the former head of the Division of National Mapping.

4 November 1988: Lecture for the Opening of Olympic Dam

Len was invited by the Western Mining Corporation to be the guest speaker at a function held at the Hyatt Regency, Adelaide, to commemorate the opening of the Olympic Dam uranium mine in far north South Australia.

15 February 1989: Advance Australia Award

Len's nomination for this award was organised by fellow churchgoer and old friend, Clem Smith. The award, in the form of a chrome-plated metal trophy, was presented by the Governor of South Australia, Sir Donald Dunstan, at a ceremony at Government House.

Len (far right) and Connie (centre, back) with a group of friends at the 'centre of gravity of Australia,' July 1991.

Len and other recipients of the Advance Australia Awards, with the Governor of South Australia, Sir Donald Dunstan (centre), February 1989.

Len receives the Order of Australia from Sir Donald Dunstan, May 1989.

Len demonstrates how a theodolite works, at the 250-mile centreline post during filming of the video Too Long In The Bush, *May/June 1991.*

9 May 1989: Order of Australia (OAM)

Len was again at Government House three months later, this time being presented with the Medal of the Order of Australia by Sir Donald Dunstan. By now, Sir Donald knew Len well. He quipped to Len: 'We've got to stop meeting like this!' Len wore a dark green suit and desert boots for the occasion. The OAM award was first announced as part of the Queen's Birthday Honours list on 13 June the previous year. Jenny Freeman from Frenchs Forrest, New South Wales, was responsible for organising Len's nomination, which included letters of support from *inter alia* Sir Mark Oliphant, Hon Bruce Eastick, Harry Butler, Jack Absalom, Hans Tholstrup and Dick Lang.

July 1989: Author's Tour of Australia

Weldon Publishing secured the publishing rights to Len's six books from Lansdowne Rigby in 1989. New covers, featuring photos by Leo Meier and Reg Morrison, were designed for each book. A limited edition (1 000) boxed set, comprising all six of Len's books, was printed, as were individual titles. Len undertook a one-week whirlwind author's tour of Australia in the last week of July to promote the release of his books. He visited Sydney, Brisbane, Melbourne and Adelaide in rapid succession and held interviews with media personalities including Ray Martin, the late Andrew Ollie, Don Willesee, Joan McInnes, Phillip Adams, Jeremy Cordeaux and Ian McNamara.

4-6 May 1990: 50th Reunion of the 2nd Australian Field Survey Company

Len was reunited with many of his colleagues from the war years during the 50th Reunion of the 2nd Australian Field Survey Company AIF (Royal Australian Survey Corps) at Dungog, New South Wales. Dungog was the site at which the Survey Corps were originally trained for overseas combat.

May/June 1991: The Video *Too Long In The Bush*

Adelaide film-maker Phil Sexton first met Len at his Salisbury home in June 1988, soon after the Queen's Birthday Honours list had been announced. Phil was filming an interview with Len on his OAM award for local television news. He proposed the concept of making a video documentary about Len's work in opening up the Australian deserts. Len had been made such an offer many times before without fruition, but this time the idea became a reality.

Len and Anne headed off into the bush with Phil and sound recordist Steve Holden on 30 May 1991. Dick and Helen Lang accompanied the team for the first night. Rover Australia generously provided Len with a new Land Rover Discovery for the project.

Filming was completed over a two-week period. After heading west from Alice Springs, footage was shot at locations including Sandy Blight Junction, Giles, Mt Beadell, Emu and the 250-mile centreline point. Heavy rain around Warburton precluded filming along the Connie Sue Highway.

The 50-minute video was released for sale in October 1993 and provides a lasting record of Len's achievements in the Australian bush.

30 April 1993: Len's 70th Birthday Party

Len's 70th birthday was celebrated with a gathering of friends and family at Trinity College, Gawler, north of Adelaide. The party was organised by daughter Jacqui and provided a memorable evening of non-stop laughter. Long-time friends including John Whitehouse and Jimmy Owens, Reverend Alan Courtney, Suzie Vickers (WRE days), Dick Lang, Rex Ellis and Peter Vernon all shared humorous anecdotes about Len's life. Laurel and Jim Pinkerton ventured all the way from Monto in Queensland to attend. Others included Kevin Whisson (from the army days), Lance and Betty Anderson and Pat Finch (fellow DSTO workers).

Len with Connie and Anne at his 70th birthday party.

18 June 1994: Australian Geographic Society's Adventurer of the Year

In June 1994 Len was honoured as the Adventurer of the Year at the Australian Geographic Society's Eighth Annual Awards Night. The glittering function was held at the Sydney Convention and Exhibition Centre, Darling Harbour. Len was presented with the Society's Gold Medallion in recognition of 'his enthusiasm and energy in opening Australia's interior.'

Len received a further pleasant surprise after the function, when he renewed acquaintances with Ray Sim, a former colleague from the Australian Army Survey Corps. The pair had not seen each other for 50 years. Ironically, Ray, a talented artist, also received an award at the ceremony – for the best illustration in *Australian Geographic* in 1993.

Len and Anne spent the next weekend as house guests of Dick and Pip Smith. Len and Dick talked for hours as they poured over maps of the Australian deserts.

11 March 1995: Len's Last Lecture

Len presented his last lecture to an audience attending an Athletic and Recreational Outdoor function at Jamestown in South Australia's mid north on 11 March 1995. Len's speaking career spanned some 31 years, during which time he gave a total of around 940 lectures.

12 May 1995: Len's Final Day – Back to the Desert for Eternal Peace

At 36 minutes past midnight on Friday 12 May 1995, Len Beadell died at the Lyell McEwin Hospital, Elizabeth Vale, Adelaide.

Len first experienced heart problems in December 1990 when he fainted in church and spent a night in the Lyell McEwin Hospital. In September 1992 Len became ill while at Neale Junction on a Russell Guest tour to the Great Victoria Desert. He was driven hurriedly to the Cook Hospital and then flown to Port Augusta.

Len underwent a series of medical tests at the Royal Adelaide Hospital in June 1993. He suffered severe bouts of breathlessness the following month, during a desert trip with Anne, Gary, Connie and friends Ruth and George Aspley to replace the signpost at Neale Junction. He underwent major heart surgery at the Royal Adelaide Hospital on 30 September 1993.

During April 1995 Len's health deteriorated significantly and he died the following month.

Len's wife, Anne, stated at his funeral: 'During Easter, Len came down with what we thought was the 'flu. But unfortunately it wasn't that simple and he had contracted an infection in the heart valve which had been replaced in 1993. He was fed lots of antibiotics and he hated being 'tied to that jolly Christmas tree,' as he called it. Unfortunately things deteriorated. However, he was as tenacious in confronting death as he had been in life. He fought on as long as possible; it was as if he was still looking for the right camp site to finally rest ... and those of you who camped with Lenny knew just how fussy he was about them ...'

Len's ashes were placed under a rock cairn near Woomera.

Chapter 14

*L*EN'S MEMORY LIVES ON

T HERE is no doubt that the spirit of Len Beadell will live
forever in the vast open spaces of the Gibson, Great
Victoria, Little Sandy and Great Sandy Deserts of Australia.
Permanent reminders of Len's pioneering work remain on show
for all those travellers who visit these deserts. They bear
testament to his iron-will, fortitude and dedication in opening up
the Western Deserts.

Mt Beadell

M T Beadell in the Gibson Desert is the most well-known
landmark commemorating Len. Standing an impressive 527
metres, Mt Beadell is situated on the Gunbarrel Highway, 155
kilometres west of Jackie Junction and 295 kilometres east of
Carnegie. Geologically, it is a sandstone and quartzite-capped
ochre-based hill, with a prominent, arresting red northern bluff
which provides commanding views in all directions, especially
along the full length of the Browne Range.

Len first undertook a reconnaissance of the country between Mt
Harvest (near Jackie Junction) and Carnegie, along the future
route of the Gunbarrel Highway, in May 1958. He was accompanied by a team including Bill Johnson, a senior surveyor with
the Division of National Mapping, Trevor Nossiter, a chief
surveyor at WRE, and Walter MacDougall, a Native Patrol Officer.

Bill Johnson, who had known Len since his army years, wrote
to the Director of National Mapping following this initial reconnaissance. He recommended that a prominent hill in the region
by given the name of Mt Beadell, in honour of Len. He also
requested that names including Mt Nossiter and Mt William
Lambert be adopted for other hills which had been sighted during

Mark Sheppard

Len and Anne at Mt Beadell in the Gibson Desert.

Anne Beadell admires the impressive view from the top of Mt Beadell.

Mark Sheppard

THE SHEER BREATH TAKING
BEAUTY BRINGS TEARS
TO YOUR EYES

(MT BEADELL)

the reconnaissance.

The Director of National Mapping subsequently took Johnson's recommendations to the Surveyor General of Western Australia and the name of Mt Beadell was formally approved on 20 August 1958.

John Coles (WRE and Australian Survey Office), Ray Campbell (WRE) and Ted Evans (National Mapping) positioned a station mark and beacon (NMF 20) on the top of Mt Beadell in May 1959. A pudding-shaped stone cairn was then built around this site. The exact location of the station mark is latitude 25° 32' 12.8904" S and longitude 125° 16' 27.6203" E. The mark itself is a 13mm copper tube set in concrete. The beacon is a 3.35m by 10cm by 10cm oregon pole and sits in the centre of the rock cairn, which is 2.28m in diameter and 1.83m high. Four vanes, 0.91m by 0.60m, are set 6cm below the top of the pole.

John Coles and his son, Johnny, revisited the cairn at Mt Beadell in September 1986. They cemented a small aluminium plaque at the base of the cairn, which stated in part:

Mt Beadell NMF/20, Australian Height Datum 526.98m, Named after Len Beadell BEM, surveyor, author and bushman who gave the Gunbarrel Highway its name.

Memorial at Mt Beadell

O N 12 May 1996, exactly twelve months to the day after Len passed away, over 170 people gathered at Mt Beadell for a ceremony to unveil a memorial to Len's tireless road-building exploits. The memorial was the brainchild of Ray Ferguson, a former President of the Queensland Association of Four Wheel Drive Clubs. The project received strong support from the Australian National Four Wheel Drive Council, of which Len was Patron.

The memorial comprises a 1.8m stainless-steel replica of a theodolite (Len's most treasured surveying tool), a plaque and an information board. Three days of back-breaking work, one tonne of concrete mix and 200 litres of water were required to construct the memorial. The theodolite stands on a concrete slab and is enclosed by a strong wire mesh cage with a corrugated iron roof. The plaque is embedded in the concrete base between the legs of the theodolite and inscribed as follows:

In memory of Len Beadell OAM, BEM, FIEMS (Aust) 1923-1995, Patron Australian National Four Wheel Drive Council, A Real Pioneer, Erected 12 May 1996.

Small stones from the top of Mt Beadell were impregnated into the concrete slab. The covered information board features details about Len and his network of roads. It also lists the 20 organisations which sponsored the memorial.

The monument was unveiled officially by Anne Beadell, following speeches by Ray Ferguson, Ian Lacey (President of the National Four Wheel Council), Milton Good (Northern Territory), and Ian Ward (representing the Warakurna Aboriginal Community and the Ngaanyatjarra Council). Ian was one of four Aboriginal Council members from Warakurna who were present. Anne was handed a book listing the names of all those attending the ceremony. Len's daughters Jacqui and Connie were also at the unveiling. Jacqui was accompanied by husband Russell, and Len's grandchildren, Mitchell and Courtney. The monument now stands conspicuously on Mt Beadell and provides a fitting tribute to the life and work of a truly remarkable Australian.

Beadell's Mallee

A NEW subspecies of a mallee eucalypt was first described in 1997 by respected Adelaide botanist Dean Nicolle. Dean discovered the rare mallee on 26 September 1993 near the junction of the Cook to Vokes Hill Corner Road and the Oak Valley to Tjuntjuntjara Road in the southern Great Victoria Desert. He named it Beadell's Mallee *Eucalyptus canescens beadellii.*

Dean described why he decided to name the tree after Len.

I N 1990 I decided to search for Ramel's Mallee, a eucalypt that had not been recorded since its discovery in 1876 by Ernest Giles during his crossing of Australia. Giles discovered the mallee 'beyond the Alfred and Marie Range,' which he named.

I had read some of Len's books and decided to phone him to obtain first-hand information about the Alfred and Marie Range. Len was very interested in my search and invited my parents and I to visit him at his home to discuss the expedition.

Within a week we were with Len and Anne having a cuppa at their Salisbury home. We were treated like long-lost friends. Dad and I were novices when it came to outback travel and Len's advice and knowledge was invaluable in the planning of our trip.

A few weeks before we left on our expedition in October 1990, Len and Anne called into our Reynella home to wish us well.

We reached the Alfred and Marie Range, which is situated about 100km north of Mt Beadell, but did not find the mallee. While on top of the range, we decided to plan a new trip involving a walk west from the Alfred and Marie Range to the Gary Highway. We began planning our walk on our return to Adelaide. We again visited Len and this time he gave us information on the Gary

Highway and the Anne Beadell Highway. In April 1991 we walked across the Gibson Desert to the Gary Highway, following what we imagined was Giles' original route. Again we did not find the mallee. In late 1991 an amateur botanist rediscovered Ramel's Mallee in the Little Sandy Desert some 600km beyond the Alfred and Marie Range.

In subsequent years I contacted Len on various occasions for information on tracks and localities and I have travelled on many of his roads in South Australia, Western Australia and the Northern Territory. His detailed knowledge and ability to recall almost insignificant features along Outback tracks was astounding and greatly appreciated. I remember Len fondly as a friend.

While travelling north from Cook, I discovered a new subspecies of mallee eucalypt and decided to name it after Len. The new subspecies would probably still remain undiscovered if not for Len's road.

A full description of Beadell's Mallee may be found in Dean's recently-published book *Eucalypts of South Australia*, page 110-111, as well as in an article written by Dean in *Nuytsia*, the journal of the Western Australian Herbarium (Volume 11, pages 365-382, 1997). Selected information about Beadell's Mallee is reproduced from these sources.

B EADELL'S Mallee is two to four metres tall. The bark is rough over the lower half of the stems, loose, flaky and grey-brown. The twigs possess pith glands and are non-glaucous. The adult leaves are ovate to broad-lanceolate, dull to slightly glossy and green. The buds and fruits are non-glaucous, occurring in umbrels of seven. The operculum (cap) is ribbed, rounded and clearly wider than the bud base at the join. Fruits are 12 to 14mm long by 11 to 13mm wide, with four or five valves. The flowers are cream. Seeds are glossy, red-brown.

Beadell's Mallee presently has a very restricted distribution. It is known only from a sandplain in the vicinity of the junction of the Cook to Vokes Hill Corner Road and the Oak Valley track north of Cook, where it is part of a mallee community in deep red sand in level country.   Associated species include *Eucalyptus wyolensis, E. concinna, E. eucentrica, E. pimpiniana* and *E. yumbarrana* with an understorey mainly of *Triodia* (spinifex).

Beadell's Mallee is similar to *E. canescens subsp. canescens*, but is completely non-glaucous and has green rather than grey leaves giving the whole mallee a green rather than blue-grey appearance.   Although it currently has a known distribution of only a few square kilometres, Beadell's Mallee is likely to be more widespread in other remote and inaccessible parts of the Great Victoria Desert of similar sandplain habitat.

Beadell's Mallee, named by Adelaide botanist Dean Nicolle in honour of Len.

Buds and mature fruits of Beadell's Mallee.

Lenny's Cat Cage

A FTER the completion of Len's road-building activities in November 1963, the Gunbarrel Road Construction Party's grader, a Caterpillar No 12 Model S8T, was put out to pasture at Giles Weather Station. Thereafter it was used for occasional grading work around Giles. However, for most of the time, it remained idle and exposed to the harsh elements of nature.

In 1988 David Field, a Warrant Officer with the army's Maintenance Engineering Agency in Melbourne, devised a project to provide the Caterpillar grader with a new and permanently sheltered home at Giles. David contacted Len who was delighted with the concept. The exercise became an official army bicentennial Project, known as Lenny's Cat Cage. The plans for

Carmel Sears

Len proudly drives the Gunbarrel grader into its new permanent home, 'Lenny's Cat Cage', built by members of the army's Maintenance Engineering Agency as a bicentennial Project in 1988.

Mark Shephard

The Gunbarrel Road Construction Party's grader came to rest at Giles, after grading more than 30 000 kilometres of roads through outback Australia in the 1950-60s.

the cage were drawn by Warrant Officer Darren Sinclair, David's 2IC. Sponsors were sourced and approval to erect the shelter was obtained from both the Adelaide Bureau of Meteorology and the local Aboriginal Community at Warakurna.

In late July, David and seven other members of the Maintenance Engineering Agency loaded all the equipment and raw materials required for construction of the cage into one Mack Cargo and two Unimog trucks; they then headed to Adelaide to visit Len en route to Giles.

The cage was built from strong wire mesh and covered with a corrugated iron roof. The grader itself was given a real spit polish. David explains: 'We washed and scrubbed the grader using gamolin (a detergent-based product) and water. Countless layers of grease and dirt were scrapped off the grader using "Icy Pole" sticks to ensure the paintwork wasn't scratched or damaged. We then applied dozens of coats of clear lacquer to seal the finished product. Three plaques were mounted on the grader; one from the Maintenance Engineering Agency, one from Len (see later), and one from the Australian National Four Wheel Drive Council.

Len flew to Giles on 8 August 1988. He steered the grader into its new home, before a media gathering which included cameramen from Channel 7 and the ABC and a journalist from the *Centralian Advocate*.

Today Lenny's Cat Cage remains a popular photographic stop for travellers venturing to Giles Weather Station and beyond.

As an interesting aside, the actual whereabouts of the orange hydraulic D-8 Caterpillar bulldozer used to construct the Gunbarrel Highway from Mt Davies to Carnegie remained somewhat of a mystery for many years. After the road was completed Doug Stoneham simply parked the dozer under a tree at Carnegie and left it there. Other cable D-7 bulldozers were used to build subsequent roads. The Australian Geographic Society launched a campaign to relocate the Gunbarrel bulldozer in the January 1995 issue of *Australian Geographic*. Subsequent investigations revealed that the bulldozer had been owned by several people in Western Australia's eastern goldfields before being purchased by Perth machinery dealer Arthur Zampatti. Mr Zampatti then sold the grader to Bill McLay from Dwellingup, south of Perth, in 1987. Bill, a foundation subscriber to *Australian Geographic*, saw a picture of the dozer in the magazine and immediately recognised it as his own. It had been resting idly on his 20-hectare property for three years after originally being bought for use in the construction of a dam. The dozer's authenticity was initially established by the presence of a large plate which had been bolted to the left hand side of the engine mount in the 1960s, and later verified by Doug Stoneham, the very man who drove the bulldozer during construction of the Gunbarrel Highway. Dick Smith, the founder of *Australian Geographic* and well-known entrepreneur, subsequently purchased the bulldozer from Mr McLay.

Len's Plaque on the Caterpillar Grader

'THIS Caterpillar No. 12 road grader began its active life at Australia's first atomic bomb test site at Emu in South Australia in 1953 and was later used in the development of the

Carmel Sears

Len and leader of the project, Warrant Officer David Field, stand beside two of the plaques mounted on the grader.

Maralinga nuclear testing range. From there, on the Nullarbor Plain, it was driven overland by the newly-formed Gunbarrel Road Construction Party in 1955 to spend the following eight years, to 1963, in its role of opening up for the first time 2 million square kilometres of the deserts of Central, South and Western Australia.

During this period, it graded over 6 000 kilometres of newly-bulldozed road access through the Great Victoria, Gibson and Great Sandy Deserts, starting with the original road for the establishment of the Giles Meteorological Station. As each section was graded five times, the actual distance it worked was in excess of 30 000 kilometres. This access network was initially needed for surveys in connection with the extension of the Woomera Rocket Range, the atomic tests and instrumentation for the Blue Streak satellite launch programme.

The Gunbarrel Highway has become the most widely-known of these roads, being the first east-west link across the centre of Australia.

On 22 November 1963, after dozens of replacement blades, gearbox, transmission and engine parts, this faithful workhorse came to the end of its working life at Giles and has remained here ever since.

Len Beadell
BEM, 1987

Beadell Signposts

A SERIES of aluminium-plated signposts scattered across the vast expanses of the Western Deserts are among the most long-standing and visible reminders of Len's work in the bush. Len erected the signposts to mark interesting locations or geographical features along his network of roads. Some of the aluminium plaques are nailed to bloodwood or desert oak trees or mulga posts, while others are attached by metal rods to disused petrol drums; but wherever they are found, they are widely recognised by desert travellers as the Beadell trademark or 'bush signature.'

Unfortunately, over the years, many of the aluminium signs have been either removed or vandalised. Len often expressed his disappointment at these practices and he spent considerable time preparing new signs in his shed at his Salisbury home. He would religiously check all his signposts on every desert trip and undertake on the spot restoration work where necessary.

Table 1 in the Appendix lists the location of most of Len's signposts. They remain an integral part of the history of this region.

Also locked away in more remote parts of the Great Victoria Desert are Len's brass-plated centreline or observation posts. A full description of these markers is provided in Table 5 of the Appendix.

Metal drum at the Western Australian/ South Australian border

Two of the illustrations Len drew to support the 'Tread Lightly! On Public and Private Land campaign.'

Len Beadell Discovery Road Network

JUST a few weeks before Len died, Jan Scudamore, Executive Director of 'Tread Lightly! Australia,' spoke to Len about the future preservation of his outback road network. (Tread Lightly!, a non-profit organisation, is a national land ethics programme aimed at 'creating an awareness and responsibility among recreational users of public and private land to respect and care for the environment.' Len was a strong supporter of Tread Lightly! and drew a number of illustrations to help the campaign).

Jan, who had known Len for many years, promised that 'she would do her best to ensure that current and future generations of Australians would be able to travel and access Len's roads, and that his roads would be classified and maintained.'

Through Tread Lightly!, Jan initiated the concept of a Len Beadell Discovery Road Network. She is now forming a working group to oversee the project, which is currently in its infancy. The working group will comprise representatives from land managers, Aboriginal communities, individuals, the corporate and media sectors, users, and other interested parties. Their charter will be to ensure the long-term preservation and maintenance of Len Beadell's road network, for the benefit of both future desert travellers and Aboriginal communities living along or near his roads. The input of local communities is seen as extremely important; and intended outcomes of the project include commercial opportunities for communities and the development of a better understanding of the Aboriginal history and culture of the Western Desert region. It is Jan's vision that each of Len's roads be marked by a series of 'discovery points' highlighting specific features of interest. A variety of educational material will also be used to promote track etiquette, and to increase awareness of the environment and the region's natural and human history.

Len's memory is also perpetuated well beyond the boundaries of the Australian deserts.

Beadell Asteroid

In 1987 well-known American astronomers Eugene and Carolyn Shoemaker named a newly-discovered asteroid after Len, in recognition of his road network which enabled them to access and study meteorite impact craters in Central Australia.

The asteroid has the following citation details:

Catalogue Number	:	*3161*
Name	:	*Beadell*
Principal Provisional Designation	:	*1980 TB5*
Date of Discovery	:	*9 September 1980*
Discovery Location	:	*Mt Palomar Astronomical Observatory, California*
Discoverer	:	*Carolyn Shoemaker*

Eugene, or 'Gene' as he was better known, and Carolyn were regular visitors to Australia almost every winter from the early 1980s to 1997. They befriended the Beadells and used Len's roads frequently in their search for impact craters.

In September 1986 Len, Anne and Gary Beadell travelled to the United States, where Anne and Gary were taking part in a two-week tour of Texas with the Adelaide Harmony Choir. Daughter Connie flew from London to Los Angeles to join the tour. The Beadell family stayed with the Shoemaker's at their home in Flagstaff, Arizona, after the tour, and later accompanied them on a trip to the Grand Canyon.

Tragically, Gene was killed in a head-on road accident in the Tanami Desert on 18 July 1997, during the couple's most recent visit to Australia.

Beadell Street

There are two streets in Australia named after Len, namely Beadell Street, Burton, a northern suburb of Adelaide, and Beadell Street, Monto, near Bundaberg in Queensland.

Beadell House

During the establishment of Trinity College, Gawler, north of Adelaide, in the mid 1980s, a number of College houses were given the names of prominent or notable people from the district. 'Beadell House' was officially named on 5 October 1987. The House banner features Len standing by his theodolite with Mt Beadell in the background. Len supported the House's activities diligently and always attended their annual dinners. While he was ill in hospital during the early 1990s, Len was regularly visited by members of Beadell House. The Beadell family has a special affiliation with Trinity College as daughter Jacqui had taught there for many years.

Beadell Explorers Club

A number of Explorers Clubs were established in Adelaide during the 1980s to encourage fathers and sons interested in adventuring. The Rostrevor branch of the Explorers Club was named after Len. He presented a lecture to the Beadell Explorers Club on 14 September 1990.

Len Beadell Library

In December 1997, the City of Salisbury in Adelaide decided to name its Central Branch Library building after Len Beadell. Mayor Tony Zappia stated its council had decided on the name *The Len Beadell Library* because of Len's literary achievements and the fact that he was one of Salisbury's most well-known residents.

The Len Beadell Library will be located in the hub of the Salisbury business district and was officially opened in June 1998.

Len's memory lives on ...

$\mathcal{A}$PPENDIX:
FACT FILE ON LEN'S ROADS

The following appendix provides more detailed information on Len's work and road-building activities during the period 1947 to 1963. This information was researched by Len's daughter, Connie, and gathered from Len's personal diaries and calculation books. Peter Vernon provided additional information for Table 1.

'Dying of thirst' bloodwood tree, Gunbarrel Highway.

Table 1: Len's signposts in the Western Deserts of Australia *

Road	Location	Date on Signpost	Date Signpost Erected	Latitude**	Longitude**
Anne Beadell Highway	Tallaringa Well	5 June 1951	13 November 1957	29° 01' 42"	133° 17' 04"
	Around Emu	Unknown	8 May 1959		
	Anne's Corner	1956	25 October 1957		
	Vokes Hill Corner	2 April 1962	2 or 3 April 1962	28° 33' 56"	130° 41' 05"
	SA/WA Border	April 1962	25 April 1962	28° 30' 40"	129° 00' 00"
	Neale Junction	16 August 1962	Unknown		
Connie Sue Highway	Neale Junction	16 August 1962	Unknown		
Gary Highway	Everard Junction	27 April 1963	14 August 1963		
	Windy Corner	7 August 1963	13 August 1963	23° 34' 26"	125° 11' 32"
	Gary Junction	May 1963	3 July 1963		
Gary Junction Road	12 miles W of Liebig	23 September 1960	23 September 1960		
	Sandy Blight Junction	27 August 1960	5 October 1960	23° 11' 58"	129° 33' 35"
	WA/NT Border	12 October 1960	13 October 1960	23° 10' 00"	129° 00' 00"
	206.6 mile Point	5 November 1960	6 November 1960	22° 48' 31"	126° 44' 01"
	Gary Junction	May 1963	3 July 1963		
Gunbarrel Highway	Near Mulga Park	7 October 1957	8 October 1957		
	50 miles W of Mulga Park	23 October 1957	23 October 1957	26° 11' 17"	131° 01' 54"
	110 miles W of Mulga Park	10 October 1957	11 October 1957	26° 09' 53"	130° 04' 44"
	Musgrave Park HS (Amata)	15 August 1961	15 or 16 August 1961		
	Junction with Kintore Avenue	6 June 1961	6 June 1961		

Table 1: Len's signposts in the Western Deserts of Australia * (continued)

Road	Location	Date on Signpost	Date Signpost Erected	Latitude**	Longitude**
	North of Mt Fanny	23 June 1956	Unknown	25° 20' 31"	128° 38' 24"
	Start of Sandy Blight Junction Road	31 March 1960	25 November 1960		
	Giles	9 May 1956	20 June 1956	25° 02' 07"	128° 17' 59"
	Warburton turnoff near Giles	Unknown	24 July 1958 (post) 30 November 1960 (iron replacement)		
	50 miles W of Giles	5 April 1958	5 April 1958		
	62 miles W of Giles	10 April 1958	10 April 1958		
	70 miles W of Giles	13 April 1958	13 April 1958	24° 50' 39"	127° 20' 25"
	Jackie Junction	16 August 1958	18 August 1958 (post) October 1972 (sign)	25° 42' 27"	126° 39' 47"
	Mt Samuel rockholes	Not dated	13 September 1958		
	Bloodwood tree ('100 miles to Warburton')	17 September 1958	17 September 1958		
	Everard Junction	27 April 1963	14 August 1963		
	23 miles W of Everard Junction	15 October 1958	15 October 1958		
Maralinga to Emu Road	Half-way point (60 miles) along road (blazed bulloak)	28 August 1955	23 August 1961		
	Observatory Hill	13 August 1955	3 September 1955	28° 58' 10"	132° 03' 40"

* Not all of Len's signposts remain standing today.

** Len marked latitudes and longitudes on some, but not all, of his signposts.

Table 1: Len's signposts in the Western Deserts of Australia * (continued)

Road	Location	Date on Signpost	Date Signpost Erected	Latitude**	Longitude**
Mt Davies Road	Mt Lindsay	8 August 1956	12 August 1956		
	Just south of Mt Lindsay	10 August 1956	12 August 1956	27° 03' 43"	129° 53' 04"
	Junction with Kintore Avenue	May 1961	31 July 1961		
	111 miles NW of Emu	26 June 1957	30 June 1957	27° 49' 40"	130° 54' 50"
	46 miles NW of Emu	26 July 1957	Unknown		
	Anne's Corner	1956	25 October 1957		
Kintore Avenue	Junction with Gunbarrel Highway	6 June 1961	6 June 1961		
	Junction with Mt Davies Road	May 1961	31 July 1961		
Sandy Blight Junction Road					
	Start (18 miles E of Giles)	31 March 1960	25 November 1960	25° 10' 08"	128° 32' 19"
	Ghost Gum (44 miles from Giles)	9 April 1960	9 April 1960		
	100 mile Point	12 May 1960	12 May 1960	24° 09' 47" (Sun)	
	Half-way point between Giles and SBJ	17 May 1960	18 to 20 May 1960	24° 03' 56"	128° 39' 09"
	Sir Frederick Range turnoff	19 May 1960	20 to 21 May 1960		
	140 mile Point	1 June 1960	2 June 1960	23° 49' 15"	128° 50' 40"
	WA/NT Border	10 June 1960	13 June 1960	23° 41' 43"	129° 00' 00"
	200 mile Rock	Not dated	24 June 1960		
	Tropic of Capricorn	25 June 1960	27 June 1960	23° 30' 00"	129° 20' 38"
	Tietkens' Tree (Mt Leisler)	29 June 1960	29 June 1960		
	Sandy Blight Junction	27 August 1960	5 October 1960	23° 11' 58"	129° 33' 35"

Table 1: Len's signposts in the Western Deserts of Australia * (continued)

Road	Location	Date on Signpost	Date Signpost Erected	Latitude**	Longitude**
Vokes Hill Corner to Cook Road	Vokes Hill Corner	2 April 1962	2 or 3 April 1962	28° 33' 56"	130° 41' 05"
	Waldana Well	27 September 1961	28 September 1961		
	Churina Well	15 October 1961	15 October 1961	28° 57' 46" (Sun)	
	Bringyna Well turnoff	15 October 1961	20 October 1961		
Warburton Road	"Dying of Thirst" Tree	15 March 1958	19 August 1958 or 17 May 1959	25° 49' 30" (Sun)	
Windy Corner Road (Talawana Track)	Windy Corner	7 August 1963	13 August 1963	23° 34' 26"	125° 11' 32"
	Talawana	6 November 1963	6 November 1963		

* Not all of Len's signposts remain standing today.

** Len marked latitudes and longitudes on some, but not all, of his signposts.

Mark Shephard

A blazed desert oak at the 100-mile point along the Sandy Blight Junction Road.

Everard Junction, at the meeting of the Gunbarrel and Gary Highways.

Mark Shephard

The post at the Western Australian/ Northern Territory border.

Mark Shephard

Blazed ghost gum, Sandy Blight Junction Road.

Table 2: Len's network of Outback roads - A summary of their construction

Anne Beadell Highway

End February to 10 March 1953
Track bulldozed west of Mabel Creek, past Tallaringa Well, to Emu.

29 October to 8 November 1953
Track bulldozed from 300-mile centreline point to link with track from Mabel Creek to Emu.

29 July 1957
Track from Anne's Corner to Emu bulldozed, after completing Mt Davies Road.

28 to 29 October 1957
Conducted reconnaissance from Emu (Camera C) across 66 miles (106km) of new country to Tallaringa Well.

4 to 16 November 1957
New road graded from Emu (Camera C) to Tallaringa Well and onto Mabel Creek.

9 to 10 June 1961
Conducted reconnaissance west from Anne's Corner to Vokes Hill area.

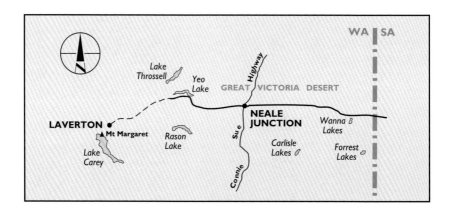

24 to 29 August 1961
Conducted a second reconnaissance west from near Anne's
Corner and found Vokes Hill on 28 August.
1 to 22 September 1961
Constructed road from Anne's Corner area to Vokes Hill
Corner.
2 April to 7 May 1962
Constructed road from Vokes Hill Corner to a point 57.5
miles (93kms) west of the SA/WA border.
9 to 11 July 1962
Reconnaissance east of Neale Junction (continuing from
earlier reconnaissance south from Warburton). Anne and
Connie accompanied Len.
14 to 24 July 1962
Reconnaissance west to Laverton with Anne and Connie.
16 August 1962
Road from west of SA/WT border to Neale Junction
completed.
10 to 17 November 1962
Road from Neale Junction to Yeo Lake completed (graded
only, not bulldozed). A sandalwood cutter's track linked Yeo
Lake to Laverton.

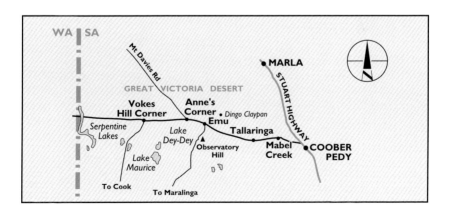

Connie Sue Highway

3 July 1962
Began reconnaissance south from Warburton (accompanied
by Anne and Connie). Future site of Neale Junction was
reached approximately 200 miles (315kms) south of
Warburton. Len then headed east to link with GRCP on 11
July.

16 August 1962
Full party arrived at Neale Junction. Construction of road
north to Warburton began.

15 September 1962
Arrived at Warburton. Northern half of Connie Sue
completed.

27 September 1962
Back at Neale Junction to start building road south to
Rawlinna.

23 October 1962
Arrived at Rawlinna. Southern half of Connie Sue completed.

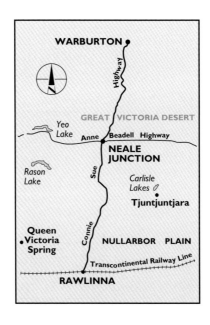

Gary Highway

27 April 1963
Party left Everard Junction.
18 May 1963
Party arrived at Gary Junction. (This road was graded only, not bulldozed).

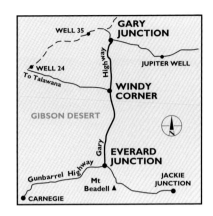

Gary Junction Road

27 August 1960
Left Sandy Blight Junction, heading east to Liebig.
16 September 1960
Road reached station tracks at Liebig.
5 October 1960
Left Sandy Blight Junction, heading west.
7 November 1960
Road reached future site of Jupiter Well.
18 to 23 May 1963
Constructed road from Gary Junction east to Jupiter Well (using grader only).
4 to 21 July 1963
Constructed road from Gary Junction west to Callawa (using grader only).

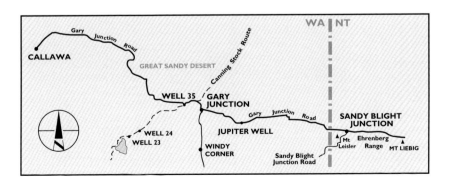

Gunbarrel Highway

13 November 1955
Party began road construction at Victory Downs.
2 December 1955
Road reached Mulga Park Homestead.
3-4 December 1955
Ground reconnaissance to Mt Davies.
7 December 1955
Aerial reconnaissance of Rawlinson Range to select future site
for weather station (Giles).
12 December 1955
Site for Giles selected, after ground reconnaissance from Mt
Davies to Rawlinson Range.
7-28 February 1956
Constructed road from Mulga Park to Mt Davies.
7-29 March 1956
Constructed road from Mt Davies to Giles.
12-15 March 1958
Len conducted reconnaissance from Giles to Warburton and
nearly died of thirst en route.
22 March - 10 May 1958
Constructed road from Giles to Jackie Junction.
14-28 May 1958
Reconnaissance from Jackie Junction to Carnegie.
18-28 August 1958
Constructed road from Jackie Junction to Warburton.
3 September - 15 November 1958
Constructed road from Jackie Junction to Carnegie.

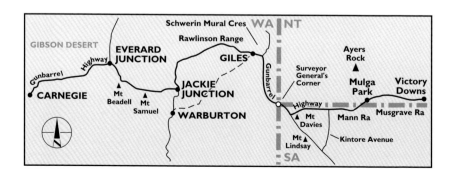

Maralinga to Emu Road

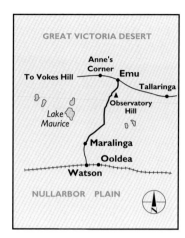

4 October 1953
Began reconnaissance to
select future site of Maralinga.
Site chosen 20 miles (35km)
NNW of Watson on
Transcontinental Railway line.
14 to 20 February 1954
Road initially bulldozed from
Maralinga area to Watson.
24 February to 12 March 1955
Constructed road from
Watson to Maralinga area.
11 August 1955
Began reconnaissance for road from Maralinga to Emu.
19 August to 17 September 1955
Interrupted construction of road from Maralinga to Emu.

Mt Davies Road

26 June to 6 July 1956
Reconnaissance for road from Mt Davies to Emu.
Reconnaissance interrupted due to mechanical problems.
23 July to 7 September 1956
170 miles (277km) of road constructed from Mt Davies SE
towards Emu. This work was conducted over two periods;
namely 23 July to 28 August (150 miles [241km]) and 2 to 7
September.
27 June - 29 July 1957
Road construction continued and reached the future site of
Anne's Corner.

Kintore Avenue

10 May - 6 June 1961
Road constructed from south-east of Mt Lindsay on the Mt Davies Road, linking with the Gunbarrel Highway near the Mann Range.

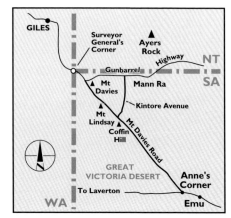

Sandy Blight Junction Road

27-29 March 1960
Reconnaissance from Giles to the Walter James Range.
31 March 1960
Road construction started from 18 miles (30km) east of Giles.
27 April - 1 May 1960
Reconnaissance around Lake Hopkins area.
19 May 1960
Constructed access road to top of Sir Frederick Range.
22-23 June 1960
Reconnaissance around Davenport Hills.
25-26 June 1960
Reconnaissance around Mt Leisler.
4 July 1960
Construction reached Sandy Blight Junction area. Further 16 miles (26km) of road constructed but never used.
27 August 1960
Site selected for Sandy Blight Junction

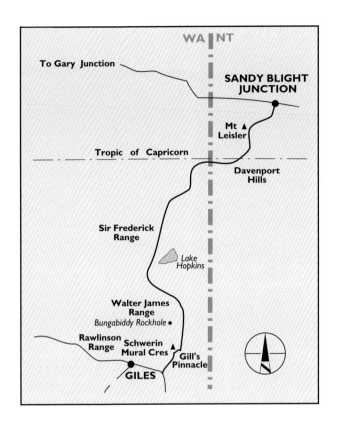

Vokes Hill Corner to Cook Road

23 September 1961
Start of construction of road south from Vokes Hill Corner.

20 November 1961
GRCP arrived at Cook. Len left the party twice during road construction (from 1 to 14 October and 8 to 17 November) to return to Adelaide where he visited Anne, who was expecting their first child, Connie.

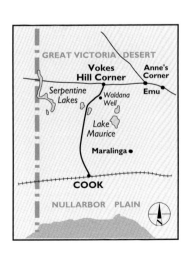

Windy Corner Road (Talawana Track)

2 August 1963
Began reconnaissance east from Talawana.
5 August 1963
Reached Curara Soaks (Well 24 on the Canning Stock Route).
7 August 1963
Intersected Gary Highway (at a site which Len called Windy Corner).
12 August 1963
Started construction of road from Windy Corner west. A broken clutch on grader halted construction. The grader was towed 220 miles (350km) to Giles.
24 September 1963
Road construction west from Windy Corner recommenced (grader only).
3 October 1963
Grader gearbox seized and construction stopped again.
30 October to 6 November 1963
Final section of Windy Corner Road to Talawana completed.

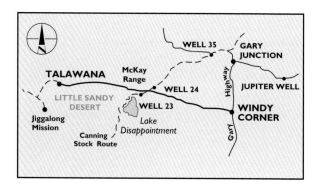

Table 3: Beadell Tracks – original distances

Road	Distance (km)*
Anne Beadell Highway (Coober Pedy to Laverton) **	1350
Connie Sue Highway	681
Gary Highway	337
Gary Junction Road (Liebig to Callawa)	1350
Gunbarrel Highway	1347
Emu to Maralinga	240
Mt Davies Road	418
Kintore Avenue	158
Sandy Blight Junction Road	377
Vokes Hill Corner to Cook Road	290
Windy Corner Road	451

*as marked on Len's signposts and converted to kilometres. These distances were taken from the speedometer readings of Len's Land Rover and represent the original routes of his roads. In some cases, they differ from the road distances of today.
**the distance from Mabel Creek to Bonny's Hut is 1066 km.

Table 4: Some latitudes and longitudes recorded by Len during field work

Location	Latitude	Longitude	Date
Carnegie HS	25° 47' 57"	122° 58' 30"	28 May 1958
Dingo Native Well	-	132° 29' 16"	10 June 1951
Dingo Claypan	28° 27' 35"	132° 30' 32"	23 June 1951
Emu Claypan	28° 37' 25"	132° 11' 24"	9 and 17 Nov 1952
Koonunda Native Well	29° 01' 37"	132° 22' 21"	9 August 1952
Mabel Creek HS	28° 56' 28"	134° 19' 23"	-
Mulga Park HS	25° 54' 20"	131° 40' 06"	7 October 1957
Musgrave Park HS	26° 08' 54"	131° 08' 48"	15 August 1961
Tallaringa Well	29° 01' 46" (sun)	-	3 June 1951
Victory Downs HS	25° 59' 15" (sun)	-	10 Nov 1955

Table 5: Len's Centreline Points, or Observation Posts

The centreline of fire for rockets launched from Woomera extended north-west from Range E, across the Great Victoria, Gibson and Great Sandy Deserts, to a point on the 80 Mile Beach, between Port Hedland and Broome on the Western Australian coast.

In 1951 Len was given the task of undertaking ground surveys to locate the centreline points at set distances from Woomera. He subsequently reached the 250, 300, 400, 500, and 550-mile points and marked their locations with a thick mulga post. A brass plate, displaying the latitude, longitude and date, was nailed onto the post. Sheets of canvas were laid out around the observation posts to ensure their location was visible from the air.

The location of the 600, 650, 700 and 800-mile points were calculated by computer, but not required to be reached by ground reconnaissance.

A. Summary of centreline points

Site	Bearing	Latitude	Longitude	Date Reached (where known)
Launching Site at Woomera – Range E	304° 42' 42"	30° 56' 37"	136° 31' 05"	
250-mile point	306° 24' 15"	28° 50' 20"	133° 07' 23"	17 June 1951
300-mile point	306° 43' 17"	28° 24' 28"	132° 27' 38"	30 June 1951
350-mile point	307° 01' 54"	27° 58' 24"	131° 48' 13"	
400-mile point	307° 20' 07"	27° 32' 09"	131° 09' 07"	16 July 1951
450-mile point	307° 37' 55"	27° 05' 43"	130° 30' 20"	
500-mile point	307° 55' 19"	26° 39' 07"	129° 51' 51"	3 August 1951
550-mile point	308° 12' 19"	26° 12' 20"	129° 13' 40"	28 July 1951
600-mile point	308° 28' 55"	25° 45' 23"	128° 35' 45"	
650-mile point	308° 45' 08"	25° 18' 15"	127° 58' 08"	
700-mile point	309° 00' 58"	24° 50' 59"	127° 20' 47"	
750-mile point	309° 16' 25"	24° 23' 33"	126° 43' 43"	
800-mile point	309° 31' 29"	23° 55' 58"	126° 06' 53"	

B. More about the centreline points

The accompanying illustrations are taken from Len's original field note book and were photographed by Beryl Mazzachi.

250-mile point

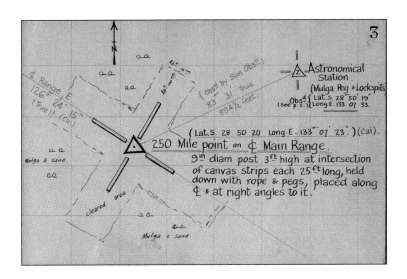

The centreline point

The mulga post is 3 feet (90cm) high and 9 inches (23cm) in diameter, with a brass plate. An area in the shape of a cross, 100 yards (91m) by 30 yards (27m), was cleared around the post. Canvas strips, 25 feet (7.6m) long, were positioned at right angles to the post and held in position by rope and pegs.

The Astrostation

Mulga peg and lockspits 894 feet 6 inches (273m) from the centreline point, at a bearing of 83° 31' true.

300-mile point

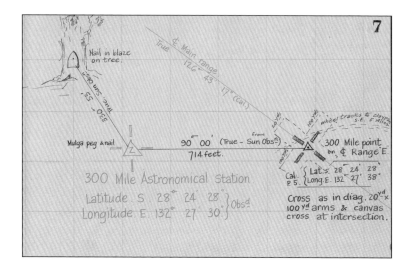

The centreline point

The original mulga post (with brass plate) was positioned on 30 June 1951. A new brass plate was attached to the post on 15 August 1951. An area in the shape of a cross, 100 yards (91m) by 20 yards (18m), was cleared around the post, and a canvas cross was laid on 12 August 1951. The original post was replaced by Len on 28 May 1993.

The Astrostation

Mulga peg and nail at 714 feet (218m) from the centreline point, at a bearing of 90° 00' true. A nail in a blaze on a tree was at a bearing of 330° 53' true from the astrostation.

Note regarding Dingo Claypan

The 300-mile point is approximately 5 miles (8km) north-west of Dingo Claypan. Len positioned a 3 foot (1 metre) mulga post with a brass plate on the northern edge of Dingo Claypan on 23 June 1951 (latitude 28° 27' 35" longitude 132° 30' 32"). When Len revisited this site with his family in 1993, the top of the post had been sawn off.

400-mile point

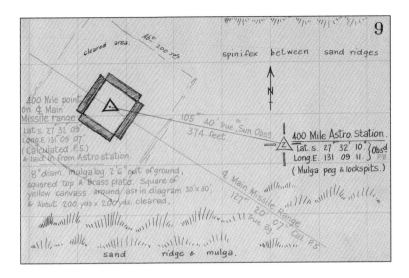

The centreline point

The square-topped mulga post is two feet six inches (76cm) high and 8 inches (20cm) in diameter, with a brass plate. The area around the post was cleared to a distance of 200 yards (180m). A 30 foot (9m) square of yellow canvas was laid out.

The Astrostation

Mulga peg and lockspits 374 feet (114m) from the centreline point, at bearing of 105° 40' true. The astrostation was refound by Len in 1991.

500-mile point

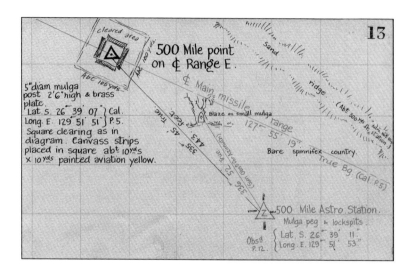

The centreline point

The mulga post is 2 feet 6 inches (76cm) high and 5 inches (13cm) in diameter, with a brass plate. The area around the post was cleared to a distance of 100 yards (91m). A 30 foot (9m) square of yellow canvas was laid out.

The Astrostation

Mulga peg and lockspits at 443 feet (135m) from the centreline point, at a bearing of 355° 45'. A small blaze on a mulga tree was made at a bearing of 336° 52' from the astrostation. A sandridge, bearing north west, is located approximately 300 yards (274m) north east of the astrostation.

550-mile point

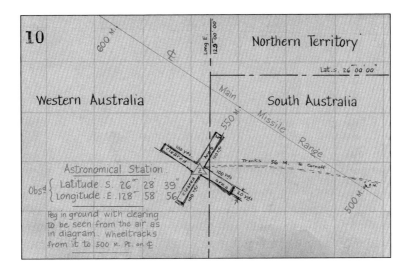

Len also reached a point 550 miles from Woomera, but offset slightly from the exact centreline of rocket fire, on 28 July 1951. He positioned a mulga peg in the ground at this location, and cleared a cross area 100 yards (91m) by 20 yards (18m) around the peg.

The newly-completed Gunbarrel Highway, Len Beadell's most famous road.

Mark Shepphard

Len's standard bush footwear - 'hobs', with no socks of course!

INDEX

Numbers in bold indicate illustration pages